TAMING THE NEXT SET OF STRATEGIC WEAPONS THREATS

Edited by
Henry Sokolski

June 2006

This book constitutes the seventh in a series of edited volumes the Nonproliferation Policy Education Center (NPEC) has produced in cooperation with the U.S. Army War College's Strategic Studies Institute(SSI). The editorial support of Marianne Cowling and Rita Rummel at the Institute made the book's production, like those before it, smooth as always. Again, my wife and NPEC's Deputy Executive Director, Amanda Sokolski, together with our assistant, Mohammad Nasseri, did the hard work in the initial preparation of the manuscript. To them, the SSI's staff, and all who helped make this book possible, NPEC and SSI are indebted.

*****

Comments pertaining to this report are invited and should be forwarded to: Director, Strategic Studies Institute, U.S. Army War College, 122 Forbes Ave, Carlisle, PA 17013-5244.

*****

All Strategic Studies Institute (SSI) monographs are available on the SSI Home-page for electronic dissemination. Hard copies of this report also may be ordered from our Homepage. SSI's Homepage address is: *www.StrategicStudiesInstitute.army.mil.*

*****

The Strategic Studies Institute publishes a monthly e-mail newsletter to update the national security community on the research of our analysts, recent and forthcoming publications, and upcoming conferences sponsored by the Institute. Each newsletter also provides a strategic commentary by one of our research analysts. If you are interested in receiving this newsletter, please subscribe on our homepage at *www.StrategicStudiesInstitute.army.mil/newsletter/newsletter.cfm.*

ISBN 1-58487-243-8

CONTENTS

INTRODUCTION

Long discounted by arms control critics, traditional nonproliferation efforts now are undergoing urgent review and reconsideration even by their supporters. Why? In large part, because the current crop of nonproliferation understandings are ill-suited to check the spread of emerging long-range missile, biological, and nuclear technologies.

Attempts to develop a legally binding inspections protocol to the Biological Weapons Convention, for example, were recently rejected by U.S. officials as being inadequate to catch serious violators while being prone to set off false alarms against perfectly innocent actors. Missile defense and unmanned air vehicle (UAV) related technologies, meanwhile, are proliferating for a variety of perfectly defensive and peaceful civilian applications. This same know-how can be used to defeat U.S. and allied air and missile defenses in new ways that are far more stressful than the existing set of ballistic missile threats. Unfortunately, the Missile Technology Control Regime (MTCR) is not yet optimized to cope with these challenges. Finally, nuclear technologies have become much more difficult to control. New centrifuge uranium enrichment facilities and relatively small fuel reprocessing plants can now be built and hidden much more readily than nuclear fuel-making plants that were operating when the Nuclear Nonproliferation Treaty (NPT) and the bulk of International Atomic Energy Agency (IAEA) inspections procedures were first devised 30 or more years ago.

This volume is designed to highlight what might happen if these emerging threats go unattended and how best to mitigate them. The book, which features research the Nonproliferation Policy Education Center commissioned, is divided into three sections. The first, *Life in a Well-Armed Crowd*, focuses on what a world proliferated with these technologies might look like. The first chapter, "Alternative Proliferation and Alliance Futures in East Asia" by Stephen Kim of the Lawrence Livermore National Laboratory, projects how the United States, Japan, Korea, and China will relate and compete with one another as each becomes more competent to deploy strategic weaponry. The good news is that further proliferation and war in the Far East are not inevitable. The bad news is that it will take considerable effort to avoid this fate.

Much is the same in the Middle East as Patrick Clawson of the Washington Institute makes clear in Chapter 2, "Proliferation in the Middle East: Who is Next after Iran?" Here, the lynch pin for further proliferation is Iran. Certainly, if Iran is able to edge toward nuclear bomb making capabilities with impunity, Tehran's neighbors are likely to hedge their security bets by developing strategic weapons options of their own.

This, then, brings us to this section's final chapter, "Nuclear 1914: The Next Big Worry." In it, I argue that the greatest security danger renewed strategic arms proliferation presents is not the increased chance of nuclear theft or terrorism, so much as the increasing difficulty small and large nations will have in determining who they can rely upon and how militarily capable they might be. In such a world, even the best plans and diplomatic hedging may be incapable of preventing miscalculation and war, much as was the case in 1914 with World War I.

The book's second section, *New Proliferation Worries*, details three of the most important emerging proliferation technology threats we face—the spread of new biological, missile, and nuclear technologies. As detailed in Mitchell Kugler's chapter, "Missile Defense Cooperation and the Missile Technology Control Regime," the United States has a clear desire to encourage missile defense cooperation with its friends and allies even though key portions of the technologies in question are restricted by the MTCR. Mr. Kugler of the Boeing Corporation makes it clear that he believes the case for sharing this technology is stronger than the case for restricting it. He believes that the MTCR should be changed to allow such commerce, or it should be put aside.

Current nuclear controls also are being challenged by emerging technology, as former U.S. Nuclear Regulatory Commissioner Victor Gilinsky makes clear in his comprehensive chapter, "A Fresh Examination of the Proliferation Dangers of Light Water Reactors." This detailed history and technical analysis of the proliferation resistance of the most popular type of power reactor concludes that the current international nuclear safeguards system needs to be modified to cope with the new risks that a proliferating state might divert the fresh or spent fuel from these machines to small, covert reprocessing or enrichment plants that could bring a state within days of having a small arsenal of weapons.

In the biological weapons threat field, current control approaches are also in desperate need of help. Dr. Allan Zelicoff explains precisely what can and is being done that can be of immediate use with health monitoring in his chapter, "Coping with Biological Threats after SARS." What is reassuring is how much public health monitoring can and has accomplished to identify and immediately treat outbreaks of infectious disease. What is challenging is how much more can and needs to be done. All of this is laid out in Dr. Zelicoff's chapter.

This brings us to the book's final section, *What Can Be Done*. In the missile technology area, Dennis Gormley and Richard Speier identify what specific new missile defense and unmanned aerial vehicle (UAV) technologies should be added to the MTCR control lists. Their chapter, "New Missiles and Models for Cooperation," also explains how the United States and other advanced states might share UAV services and turn-key missile systems rather than handing over the means for their production or, in the case of missile defenses, the countermeasures technologies needed to defeat them.

In the nuclear field, the key recommendation of the chairman of the German Bundestag's committee on energy and the environment is not to push nuclear power beyond what the market itself might otherwise demand. Certainly, if nuclear power is pushed with government subsidies too hard or too fast, there is a risk that the proliferation problems noted in Victor Gilinsky's analysis could come far sooner than the safeguards upgrades that are needed to keep them at bay. The way out here is to buy more time as Ernst Ulrich Von Weizsäcker explains in his chapter, "German Nuclear Policy." Specifically, he argues that we need to focus first on promoting the most economical way to extend energy supplies, through increased efficiencies and productivity for whatever amount of energy is available.

What are we to do with the time this might buy? In the book's concluding chapter, "President Bush's Global Nonproliferation Policy," the author details a series of steps that build on the proposals President Bush made in a February 11, 2004, speech on nuclear proliferation at the National Defense University in Washington, DC. All of these proposals deserve attention. This is especially so given the shocks the NPT and the IAEA have felt since the mid-1990s from Iraqi, North Korean, and Iranian noncompliance, Pakistan's proliferation activities under A. Q. Khan, and, most recently, the U.S. offer of civilian nuclear assistance to India, a nuclear weapons state outside of the NPT. As always, it is uncertain if we and our friends will take action. The hope is that this book and the writings of others will make clear that the price of failing to do so is sure to exceed the costs of any attempt.

SECTION I

LIFE IN A WELL-ARMED CROWD

CHAPTER 1

ALTERNATIVE PROLIFERATION
AND ALLIANCE FUTURES IN EAST ASIA

Stephen J. Kim

The gravest danger our Nation faces lies at the crossroads of radicalism and technology. Our enemies have openly declared that they are seeking weapons of mass destruction, and evidence indicates that they are doing so with determination. The United States will not allow these efforts to succeed. … History will judge harshly those who saw this coming danger but failed to act. In the new world we have entered, the only path to peace and security is the path of action.

President George Bush[1]

A central pillar of U.S. national security strategy is to control the spread of nuclear weapons. In pursuit of that objective, bilateral alliances emerge more important and pertinent than ever. If the United States and its East Asian allies can strengthen their existing bilateral relationships, and if the United States and China can come to a clearer bilateral understanding, nuclear proliferation in East Asia can be curtailed. The consequence of abandoning such alternatives could potentially be devastating.

I believe that if the United States shies away from existing treaties and alliances due to anti-American sentiments or for fear of appearing anachronistic, then doomsday exhortations will go past paranoia and become reality.[2] Anywhere from 12 to 20 nuclear powers will emerge in the next 2 decades. Terrorists and nonstate actors will exploit this worldwide proliferation as a succession of East Asian states go nuclear—North Korea, followed by South Korea, then Japan, then Taiwan.[3] An alarmed China would not sit idly by while being encircled by an island chain of democratic nuclear powers. In the absence of a strong U.S. presence and influence in East Asia, buttressed by its existing treaties and alliances, East Asia in 2025 looks bleak.

But I believe that if the United States strengthens, renews, and revamps its existing bilateral treaty alliances with Japan and South Korea, the nuclear temptation in East Asia could be dampened. That is, if the United States maintains its nuclear deterrence umbrella over Japan and South Korea, North Korea's nuclear breakout will not lead governments in Tokyo and Seoul to seek an indigenous nuclear option. Concurrent with the strengthening of existing treaties and alliances in East Asia, the United States will also need to reach a new bilateral understanding with China over the proliferation of nuclear weapons.

What We Want.

One can envision some ideal scenarios for East Asia in 2025. One can project an economically vibrant China with its nuclear capability remaining at about the current level of 35 weapons without multiple independent reentry vehicle (MIRV) capability, a unified Korea shorn of nuclear capability, a rejuvenated Japan without nuclear weapons, and a perfunctory U.S. military presence in Guam. Trade and investment issues would largely overshadow security concerns or worries about a heavy U.S. footprint in East Asia.

One can hope that by 2025, China will have abolished the *laogai*, the Chinese prison camps akin to the Soviet *gulag*, and that Japan will have thoroughly deromanticized the sentiment and philosophical rationale behind the Greater East Asian Co-Prosperity Sphere, a political, psychological, and intellectual tool wielded to great effect by Japanese militarists to justify colonial rule over Korea, Taiwan, and Manchuria.

One can hope that the 2008 Summer Olympics in Beijing will encourage reformist factions within the Chinese Communist Party (CCP). If economic growth were to continue at today's pace and if the Chinese government were to relax control over loans and property, there is a possibility that the CCP could evolve into a dominant party with various factions akin to Japan's Liberal Democratic Party (LDP). Chinese Vice Minister of Commerce Ma Xiuhong recently predicted that China will quadruple "its GDP of the year 2000 by 2020."[4]

One can hope that such a development can serve as an impetus for the emergence of a semi-democratic China by 2025. No one

4

expects U.S.-style democracy to emerge from the devolution of the CCP, but one holds out hope for a China with limited free elections and some freedom of the press. Democratic centralism could evolve along the lines envisioned by Eduard Bernstein rather than Peng Zhen and the Eight Immortals. Such expectations are not pie-in-the-sky speculations. After all, no one could have imagined in 1978 that Deng Xiaoping's China would permit Hooters restaurants to operate 26 years later in 2004, even if it is Shanghai.

China can continue to serve as a market for thriving and mature economies. Trade between India and China more than doubled between 2001 and 2003.[5] South Korean, Taiwanese, and Japanese investments in China are large and growing. Such a China would have no reason to fear Japan, a unified Korea or the presence of U.S. forces in East Asia.

One can hope that North Korea does not exist by 2025. One may hope that North Korea implodes from within (due to some critical external pressures) and that a benign military dictatorship assumes power after the fall of Kim Jong Il. If China blocks its 800-km border with North Korea and the United States and South Korea maintain the Demilitarized Zone (DMZ), the fear of millions of refugees pouring into Seoul or northern China would dissipate. China fears North Korean refugees due to the potential ramifications for its own regime security arising from the social and economic instability the refugees might bring.

One can imagine that new investments from South Korea, Japan, China, Australia, the European Union (EU), and the United States could pour into this "refugee-contained" North Korea teeming with a large pool of literate, skilled, and cheap North Koreans eager for work and real wages. Nongovernmental organizations and programs (i.e., the United Nations [UN] and the World Food Program) would continue to dispense humanitarian and food aid. Given its cultural and linguistical ties, South Korea could take the lead in these initiatives by promising 200 tons of rice every year, a pittance for the country.

As for reunification, one holds out the hope that the new leadership would elect to unify peacefully with a prosperous South Korea into a single democratic Korea, tied firmly to the United States, if not militarily then economically.[6] There are two schools of thought on Korean unification. The first school emphasizes that Koreans are one people of a singular culture. In this view, economic difficulties of unification are secondary to physical unification. The second school holds that South Korea will absorb North Korea. In this view, North Korea's nuclear weapons will merely fall into the lap of a unified Korea, and the resultant large pool of labor would be used to compete with an emerging China. Both of these schools of thought are anchored on the optimistic assumption that South Korea would take the lead — with its democracy, free markets, wealth, and freedom.

One can hope that Japan faces up to its colonial and imperial past, apologizes unequivocally once and for all to Koreans, Chinese, Taiwanese and Filipinos, and suppresses its expansionist nationalism. One hopes that there shall be no nostalgia for the Kwantung Army mentality among military leaders, no reversion to the hesitation and weakness of the Fumimaro Konoe government, and no repeat of any whiff of a Marco Polo Bridge incident in July 1937 to justify the advancement of any irrendentist or revanchistic goals. One hopes Japan will emerge as a "normal" country, amending its pacifist Constitution without alarming its neighbors.[7]

This "new" Japan would continue to welcome U.S. forces without striving for nuclear capability. Chief Cabinet Secretary Yasuo Fukuda made an impassioned argument against Japan going nuclear: "Currently, Japan need not, and should not, have a nuclear deterrent. Japan having such arms would be a threat to other countries, and it would be tragic if that led to (further) nuclear proliferation."[8] For the time being, Fukuda's argument still holds sway in the LDP establishment and the general public. With a rejuvenated economy, Japan would be able to spread its capital and wealth throughout a unified Korea, China, and the world markets. That would be some East Asia.

What We Do Not Want.

But what about alternative futures we do not want to see in 2025? It is easier to be a pessimist because one has selective recourse to the data of history. One remains anxious as to whether the lure of past glory and regional predominance tugs at the heart of Chinese or Japanese leaders. In their long histories, China has rarely been democratic; Japan has rarely been pacifistic; Korea has rarely been unhindered by great power conflicts. The withdrawal of U.S. forces that would accompany the abrogation of our treaty and alliance commitments in East Asia would likely harbinger a future reeking with the unpleasantness and chauvinism of East Asia's past.

Rather than serving as a rally point for reform and genuine opening of the society, the 2008 Beijing Olympic games could be used as a bugle for Chinese nationalism. If the United States and China fail to reach a clear understanding about nuclear proliferation, the withdrawal of U.S. forces from South Korea and Japan will only embolden a confident and assertive China. Chinese nationalists will want to throw their weight around East Asia. In this environment, I believe that as soon as China achieves domestic stability, it will try to penetrate culturally into neighboring countries. The Chin, Sui, Tang, and Qing dynasties were not exceptions. As soon as it feels that it has achieved its original target for economic reforms, and buttressed by its confident nationalistic impulses, China is likely to claim, at a minimum, its regional power hegemony in East Asia.[9]

The next generation of Chinese nationalist leaders suffers little in confidence, panache, or assertiveness. On May 7, 1999, during Operation ALLIED FORCE, U.S. forces mistakenly struck the Chinese Embassy in Belgrade. The young Chinese vice president condemned the bombing and "allowed" anti-U.S. demonstrations. He argued that these demonstrations "fully reflect the Chinese people's great fury at the atrocity of the embassy attacks by NATO [the North Atlantic Treaty Organization] and the Chinese people's strong patriotism."[10] The voice belonged to none other than Hu Jintao.

The October 15, 2004, launching of *Shenzhou V* to space is a source of great national pride in China. Lieutenant Colonel Yang Liwei is a hero.[11] One suspects that China will forge ahead aggressively with is space program as well as attempt to acquire MIRV capability by 2025. Even as it faces rising unemployment, the Chinese military has announced its intention to modernize the People's Liberation Army (PLA) for the 21st century. A China insecure about the "three Ts"—Taiwan, Tibet, and Tiananmen—will mean a more threatening, paranoid China.[12]

Japan has begun to "talk" about the possession of nuclear weapons. That in itself may signal a portentous change. One fears that if the United States is lukewarm in sharing high-tech conventional capabilities or back-pedals on promises to share missile defense technology, Japanese nationalists will clamor for an independent nuclear capability.[13] Kenzo Yoneda has been especially vocal in challenging the nuclear "taboo," arguing that the United States may not automatically and unconditionally come to wield its sword in defense of Japan.[14]

Defense Minister Shigeru Ishiba pushes aggressively for missile defense cooperation with the United States, and young politicians petition for a new security system for the new century.[15] Deputy Chief Cabinet Secretary Shinzo Abe has stated that Japan needs to rethink its fundamental values as a nation.[16]

The apotheosis of Japanese conservative nationalism, Tokyo Governor Shintaro Ishihara, has insulted China by ridiculing its recent space flight: "The Chinese are ignorant, so they're overjoyed. That (spaceship) was an outdated one. If Japan wanted to do it, we could do it in 1 year." In the same week, Ishihara insulted his other Asian neighbor. Resuscitating the "arrogance" of Japanese imperialism, Ishihara said Koreans chose Japanese annexation of their country in 1910. Ishihara added salt to the Korean wound: ". . . the annexation was the fault of their ancestors, and even though Japan's rule was in the form of colonialism, it was advanced and humanitarian."[17] No one has yet heard strong condemnation of these remarks from prominent Japanese politicians and academics.

Other ominous signs of Japanese nationalism are the rapid growth of youth nationalist societies, some of which have inserted themselves in the island disputes between Japan and China on the South China Sea, especially over the Senkaku Islands (Diaoyu Tai). Due to the North Korean threat, the general mood in Japan is one of a terrified atmosphere, a feeling of powerlessness. Reports of "North Korean guided missiles threaten Japan" are plastered everywhere. There is a feeling of chaos, that civilian leaders are not up to the challenges of the times—with uncomfortable echoes of a leaderless, drifting Japan of the Taisho period of the 1920s and 1930s. Japanese nationalists are and will continue to gain political and social ground in Japan.

One fears that the North Korean problem will exacerbate. North Korea may not collapse. Though some 8-10 percent of its 22 million population have starved to death or have fled, there are little overt signs that the regime will collapse any time soon, though the strength of its stability may be overemphasized. Many Western observers assessed that North Korea would not last beyond 5 years during the 1993-94 nuclear negotiations, and key policy decisions were made on that "mistaken" assumption. Credible reports of North Korean diversion of food and humanitarian aid to its military are coming in.[18]

By 2025, North Korea may have proven its nuclear capability to the world. A North Korean nuclear breakout is worrisome for the effect it would have on states *outside* of East Asia. Arguing that, "the only possible way for nations who want to survive proudly and live independently is to be strong and grow muscles of their own," Iran has declared, "We must believe that the proper and effective way is that which has been opted by North Korea."[19] Iran lacks neither money nor ambition, and it is only a matter of time before it acquires nuclear capability.

The normal standards of economic and moral constraints are inapplicable to North Korea. Though North Korea spends some $5.2 billion on its military, some 11 percent of its gross domestic product (GDP), it has ostensibly been able to advance its nuclear program. North Korea is considered to possess materials to make one or two nuclear weapons. Some estimate that it could produce five or six nuclear weapons in a relatively short time.[20] As worrisome as its nuclear weapons program, North Korea's advancement in ballistic missiles may be even more disturbing.[21]

There is a good chance that by 2025, North Korea may have succeeded in developing ballistic missiles (Taepo Dong II) with tighter circular error probables (CEPs) that could hit targets all across the United States. The Kim Jong Il regime may still be in power by 2025, having struck a deal with the United States to remain in power in return for inspections of some of its facilities. There could be a second succession in North Korea (see below).

The situation in South Korea could develop for the worse. If the United States tries to eliminate the remnants of the North Korean nuclear program via strike operations, young Korean nationalists will increase their anti-American rhetoric and demand the withdrawal of U.S. forces from South Korea. The "386" generation (those who are in their 30s, attended university in the 1980s, born in the 1960s) have been a political force since the Chun Doo Whan administration, but with the election of President Roh Moo Hyun in December 2002, they have entered the corridors of power.[22] The 386ers in the current administration are less inclined to rely on the United States, with some questioning the very rationale for the U.S. defense commitment. Some have espoused looking at things from a North Korean point of view.[23] Some from the *jusapa*, the National Liberation faction, are flat-out pro-North Korea.[24] The "spirit of 6.15" and the rhetoric of *han minjok* (a single unitary race) are distilled in a powerful call for the cultural and racial unity of "fellow brothers" in a unified Korea. They have unwittingly inherited the nationalistic argument from the over-confident South Korean conservatives of the 1980s who boasted that North Korean nuclear weapons should not be worrisome because "it will be ours one day" (after unification).

To be sure, there are more "conservative" 386ers.[25] But even many younger members of the opposition party, the Grand National Party (GNP), hold a skeptical view of the United States. Even as Choe Byung-Ryul called for a strengthening of U.S.-ROK alliance upon his election as party leader, Choe has surrounded himself and has at times accommodated the demands of the *Mirae Yondae*, a young reformist faction of 386ers.[26] It is uncertain at this juncture whether the new GNP chief, Park Geun Hae, has consolidated support of these "conservative" 386ers within the GNP. Despite the nominal political differences, the next generations of Koreans glamorize an autonomous republic, independent of the United States, a foreign policy utopia fueled by President Roh Moo Hyun.[27] Many members of this generation consider the United States to be "most threatening to the ROK (Republic of Korea)" after North Korea.[28] Regardless of their political inclinations, the nationalistic 386ers, as a political and social class, will be the dominant political force in South Korea for the next 20-30 years.

In 10-20 years time, South Korea may be "sandwiched between China, increasingly known as the 'factory of the world,' and Japan, with its cutting-edge technology."[29] Things could get worse. Soon after it gains a security guarantee, North Korea could demand the withdrawal of all foreign (i.e., U.S.) forces from the Korean peninsula. Buoyed by pro-North Korean sympathizers in South Korea, North Korea would echo the Roh Moo Hyun government's repeal of South Korea's National Security Law, on the books since 1958.

As for reunification possibilities, prospects may not be that rosy. South Korea may not be able to take the lead, let alone absorb North Korea. There could emerge a unified but weak Korea. South Korea has barely recovered from the 1997 financial crisis that required International Monies Fund (IMF) intervention. South Korea has 7 million unemployed. According to South Korean conservatives, nearly 10 percent of South Koreans are believers or sympathizers of North Korea—that is about 4 million people. In North Korea, one can reasonably surmise that some 3-4 million (those formerly in the Korean Worker's Party and the Korean People's Army) may extol the good old days of North Korean communism. Some 15 million North Koreans will likely be unemployed if the Kim regime is removed. North Koreans may at first welcome unification, but economic difficulties may lead them to reflexive nostalgia for socialism. A generation that has starved and a people who have been taught to think and behave for over 50 years will not become active participatory citizens overnight. Anyone can do the math. The democratic center, rooted in free elections and the market economy, may not hold. West Germany was a strong economic power in 1989; East Germany was the best-run country in Eastern Europe. And, still, a unified Germany underwent a very unstable period of time during which many Germans themselves and outsiders thought that the financial burden of unification could not be met.

How to Get What We Want: Alliances and Treaties.

Given our optimistic and pessimistic projections for the next 20 years or so, how does the United States go about seeking what we want? In other words, what is likely to develop in East Asia by 2025, and how does the United States mold, shape, and adjust to those anticipated developments? I argue that the strengthening of our bilateral alliance with South Korea and Japan and the forging of a new understanding with China on nuclear proliferation are the keys to shaping the East Asian future we want to confront in 2025.

At first glance, the East Asian structure seems an ill fit to tempering nuclear proliferation. Observers are quick to point out the absence of a NATO-type structure for East Asia. There are no East Asian equivalents of a Monroe Doctrine, the Rio Pact, the Organization of American States (OAS); no West European Union (WEU) political counterpart. At best, there is the now defunct South East Asian Treaty Organization (SEATO).

But on closer examination, the United States is "blessed" not to have a NATO-type organization in East Asia.[30] Critics who pinned the mistakes and shortcomings of U.S. policy in East Asia on this absence of multilateral organizational structure miss the mark. U.S. Forces Korea's (USFK) commander General Leon Laporte has more flexibility and leeway than General Lauris Norstad had at the height of Supreme Allied Command Europe's (SACEUR) prestige and responsibility. Multilateral alliances can fall victim to factionalism and disagreements over "who's turn" it is in rotation assignments and responsibilities. Bilateral alliances and treaties, on the other hand, give the United States flexibility in offering positive inducements and holding out negative consequences. If the collective sum of a multilateral alliance is its strength, then the one-on-one nature of bilateral alliances gives the United States more direct leverage over its ally and lowers the probability of misunderstanding and collusion against it. Bilateral alliances can be leveraged to pressure third parties with whom its allies have relations. Examples are not hard to find.

Despite Tokyo's insistence that the abduction issue is their top priority in negotiations with North Korea, Japan has agreed that a written security guarantee of North Korea takes precedence. Japan will "not insist on including the abduction issue" in the second round of the 6-nation talks over North Korea's nuclear program.[31]

Ostensibly, the United States also pressured Japan to not sign a $2 billion contract for Iran's oil. Shoichi Nakagawa, the new minister of economy, trade, and industry stated that Japan would treat the bilateral agreement for Iran's Azadegan oil field "in its totality," indicating that the "contract could not be separated from suspicions over Iran's nuclear programme."[32]

Anti-American sentiments reached its apex during South Korea's December 2002 Presidential election. Though hardly at its nadir today, anti-American sentiments are on the wane, due in large part to the U.S. decision to pull back frontline troops beyond the Han River, south of Seoul, as well as a well-timed announcement for possible draw down of some of its 37,000 troops stationed in South Korea.[33] The calibration of the deployment of U.S. forces will have a palpable effect on how South Korea defines its national security and decides on its defense policies. The U.S.-ROK alliance emerges as ever important in the resolution of the North Korean nuclear problem, as any potential strike operations against selective North Korean facilities would require Seoul's approval of the use of its airspace.

The United States can also dangle to Japan and South Korea the prospect of joining the 10 rotating UN Security Council memberships for their cooperation in keeping East Asia nuclear free. Algeria, the Philippines, Romania, Brazil, and Benin are to begin their term on January 1, 2004. The 2-year rotation for the other 5-member group begins on January 1, 2005.[34]

On a final note, Japan and South Korea are free, democratic, liberal, capitalistic, and open societies, and have been our allies for over 50 years. Yet the United States still does not know Japan and South Korea all *that* well. If we have shortcomings in our understandings of our East Asian allies, how do we even approach minimal understanding of our East Asian adversaries? As one observer noted: "When we confront an opponent with nuclear weapons, we misread cues, signals, threats, and responses, most of all when the opponent stands outside of Western culture. They will misread us in turn."[35] Thus, the strengthening of existing bilateral alliances gains more importance for our efforts to curb nuclear proliferation in East Asia.

Treaties.

The two pillars of post-World War II treaties — the San Francisco Peace Treaty (September 8, 1951) and the Korean Armistice Agreement (July 27, 1953) — appear outdated. Some have even called for the end of the U.S.-ROK alliance.[36] But those calling for the end of such alliances never posit what would replace them.

The abolition of these two treaties would be recognition of the restoration of Japan and South Korea to "normal" status. New treaties or agreements that would replace the San Francisco Peace

Treaty and the Korean Armistice Agreement would have to consider how Japan and South Korea would defend themselves in their new role as normal nations, nations responsible for their own defenses and which would no longer be divided.

But it seems difficult to imagine a scenario where this would occur absent the unification of Korea. Thus, the crux of the matter is what will develop on the Korean peninsula by the year 2025. The fallout of Korean unification will affect developments in Japan and China. An important factor will be how the United States confronts and manages such developments.

If Korea is unified peacefully and emerges as a single, democratic, capitalistic nation, then the armistice agreement will become moot. And if such a benign development were to occur, then the San Francisco treaty would become irrelevant. But both treaties are "holding" treaties that are buttressed by specific defense commitments in the U.S.-Japan and U.S.-ROK mutual defense treaties, the two most important alliances in East Asia.[37] The strengthening of these treaties and bilateral alliances is critical. Such buttressing sends a clear message that the United States keeps its word and adheres to its commitments. At the same time, the nature of the bilateral alliances with Japan and Korea allows the United States to be flexible.

Any revision of the mutual defense treaties will require a revision of America's nuclear umbrella over and defense commitment to South Korea and Japan. The clause allowing the deployment of U.S. forces "in and around" Japan and Korea will need to be expunged. A peace treaty in Korea will need to replace the armistice agreement, and a new treaty or agreement would need to follow the San Francisco treaty.

In light of our deep concern about proliferation, we should not be so hasty in revising or replacing these two key alliance treaties. In short, if the United States continues to provide a nuclear umbrella for the defense of Japan and South Korea, then the two nations will have a difficult justification for going nuclear.

Some have argued that a nuclear North Korea would be a sufficient threat to make Japan go nuclear, to provoke South Korea to revisit suspension of its nuclear programs in the mid-1970s, or to force China to accelerate weaponization of its nuclear materials.[38]

But despite these views, and despite the rhetoric of some politicians and officials in the United States and East Asia, I believe that Japan would *not* go nuclear even if North Korea declared itself a nuclear power or was proven to have nuclear weapons.

The underlying assumption of such a conjecture is that the status quo on the Korean peninsula will hold, that the Kim Jong Il regime will continue to persevere.[39] In 2025 Kim Jong Il will be 83 years old. There is already circumstantial evidence that a second succession is in the works. The glorification of Kim Jong Il's third wife, Koh Young Hee, has already begun. Their two sons, Jong-Chul and Jong-Un, are likely successors. A fantasy? In 1980, the same year that the glorification of his mother, Kim Jung-Sook, began in earnest, Kim Jong Il was officially anointed the successor.[40]

Kim Jong Chul works in the Operation and Guidance Department, the very same launching pad for his father's accession in 1973 when he assumed control of the same department. Kim Jong Il's first son, Jong-Nam, reportedly works in the State Security Department (SSD) but his careless attempt to enter Japan on a fake Dominican passport might have ruined his chance to succeed his father. Chang Seung-Taek, Kim Jong Il's brother-in-law, is under house arrest, similar to the isolation, marginalization, and containment of Kim Young-Ju (Kim Il Sung's brother) and Kim Pyong-Il (Kim Jong-Il's half-brother) in the early 1970s.

But I posit that the Japanese and South Korean nuclear calculus may change if Korean unification is achieved under the following circumstances: If Korea is unified via South Korean absorption of the North and if U.S. forces remain in a unified Korea, then the presence of U.S. forces may dampen the temptations of a united Korea to restart a nuclear weapons program.[41] However, if Korea is unified with the South inheriting the remnants of the North's nuclear program and a Seoul-centered, unified Korea is unwilling to abandon or freeze the program and begins to engage in irredentist rhetoric, it is highly unlikely that Japan will remain quiet.

Some have argued that Japan does not oppose a unified Korea. Others have said that Japan's real concern is China.[42] They may be peripherally right. But China already has nuclear weapons and missiles capable of reaching Japan. South Korea does not. The August 1998 *Taepo Dong* launch already had underscored Pyongyang's ability to hit all of Japan. Yet, Japan did not go nuclear. If the U.S.-Japan alliance stays intact and if a unified Korea does not abrogate the U.S.-ROK security treaty, then the Japanese nuclear temptation may be alleviated.

However, if a unified Korea acquires nuclear capability (as well as having nearly 1.8 million Koreans in arms—1.1 million North Korean and 680,000 South Korean soldiers) and decides that the United States is no longer needed for its security, then the nuclear temptation will metastasize into a critical need for Japan. If Japan confronts what it considers (still) an upstart, uppity, unitary Korea getting its hands on nuclear weapons and unconstrained by a U.S. alliance, then Japan will seek nuclear weapons capability—and seek them rapidly. Japan will never accept a Korea outpacing it, let alone one that can threaten it with nuclear diplomacy. Thus, a unified Korea with nuclear weapons, unfettered by an alliance with Washington, rather than a nuclear North Korea is the triggering point for Japan going nuclear.

China will likely continue its modernization of existing nuclear capability by seeking MIRV capability. China is also likely to pursue at full speed its space program.[43] But even this projected development depends on U.S. actions. If Korea is unified and retains nuclear capability, if the United States remains tied to such a unified Korea with troops stationed close to the Chinese border, and if Japan goes nuclear, China will become threatened. Already, China has taken precautionary steps to ensure against any undesirable American encroachment of influence over the Korean peninsula by deploying Chinese troops along the North Korean border. At the very least, Chinese leaders would prefer to have a pro-China government, compliant to its regional desiderata in a post-Kim Jong Il North Korea.

However, if nominal U.S. forces remain in Korea far from the Chinese borders, with the bulk stationed in Guam, then a delicate balance could be reached. There is no need for China to fear a unified Korea tied militarily to the United States if no U.S. troops are on its northeastern border. In this scenario, the United States will not have completely withdrawn from East Asia per se. U.S. forces will not be near Chinese territory yet not too far away to deter possible outbreak of hostile movement by China against Korea or Japan. U.S. presence in Guam will also serve as a "psychological buffer" for potential conflict between Japan and a unified Korea—even if both possess nuclear capabilities. A mobile U.S. missile defense capability and technology, along with Guam's location, will allow it to accomplish a balance of power in East Asia without withdrawal of its presence from the region.

Thus, we need to reach a very clear understanding with the Chinese about nuclear nonproliferation. As in 1994, we can pressure China to "not oppose" economic sanctions against North Korea. In the event China continues to supply North Korea with sensitive materials that could be used for its nuclear program, the United States can make clear to China that selective tariff measures could be contemplated if such activities were not halted. To be sure, such "trade wars" would hurt the U.S. economy. But it would cripple China's. The last thing Chinese leaders want at this stage is a slowdown of the *pace* of its economic growth. To be sure, Chinese leaders worry about the possibility of North Korean nuclear materials falling into the hands of pro-independence groups in Xinjiang (East Turkmenistan) to advance their separatist goals. But that problem is viewed as one among many on its periphery. The continued acceleration of its economy is central to the Chinese leaders' political epistemology. Chinese leaders view the 2008 Olympics, the 2010 Shanghai Expo, and the 2014 World Cup as the catalyst by which the Chinese economy can advance to its next huge take-off. An administration official nailed it on the head: "It is the possibility of a huge economic impact that we hope gets the attention of Chinese decisionmakers to do more on preventing WMD [weapons of mass destruction] proliferation."[44] We have broad, mature relations with China. And Chinese leaders strive for stability on its frontiers and borders so as to continue its economic development. We need to expand on that relationship and intersection of national interests to make it clear what we are prepared to overlook and what we will not tolerate.

What to Do—New Approaches.

The United States cannot remain wedded to 20th century solutions to 21st century problems. We need to question, rethink, and produce bold, sweeping approaches to the prospect of curtailing nuclear proliferation in East Asia.

The Nuclear Nonproliferation Treaty (NPT) and the UN International Atomic Energy Agency (IAEA) need to be strengthened.[45] IAEA inspections have been able to neither affirm innocence nor prove guilt in a manner that is effective in the international policy context and opinion. The set-up as it is incorporates the possibility of failure because it permits capability acquisition. I think that national will matters as much as technical ability in the pursuit of nuclear weapons. But if one were to focus specifically on technical means, I would take mild issue with those who emphasize the primacy of nuclear weapons design (important as it is). There are problems with this emphasis, not the least of which is that the IAEA mandate does not cover nuclear weapons design because nuclear weapons design is very difficult to monitor and verify. Instead, I posit that the engineering of nuclear fissile material is the critical node, the most important bellwether of the problem. Thus, we may explore the possibility of modifying the IAEA mandate to include a beefed up inspection regime, exploring the gamut of the nuclear fuel cycle. At this point, the Additional Protocols are voluntary. We may have to make Special Inspections mandatory and the norm.[46]

Related to this, we can think of ways to expand IAEA personnel to include those who can be permanently deployed overseas to undertake monitoring. We can also propose that the various national laboratories keep ready a team of scientists and country experts deployable on a 48-hour notice.

The UN Charter may need to be modified to include nonproliferation as a central tenet of its mission. The current 2-year rotation of the elected 10 members of the UN Security Council could be shortened to a year, giving more countries a voice and a responsibility on nuclear proliferation matters.

We should also think of expanding the 5-member permanent Security Council. If this is resisted, we should think of creating an Asian Security Council with the United States, China, Japan, South Korea, Russia, and Australia as members to discuss, plan, coordinate, and implement collective security measures to curb WMD proliferation. The Proliferation Security Initiative (PSI) is a good first step toward tackling the proliferation problem. We may want to formalize PSI into a treaty, as well as persuading South Korea and China to join.

We can put forth a 21st century version of a nuclear nonproliferation Lend-Lease. American and international personnel could be leased as managers or supervisors overseeing the indigenous nuclear reactors in return for opening credit pipelines to the Asian Development Bank, the World Bank, and the IMF. After all, the professed objective of such a reactor is to generate electricity.

Missile defense also can serve to *strengthen* our bilateral alliances. The U.S. nuclear deterrence/umbrella should remain but is not very useful in the absence of a full-scale war akin to the Korean War. If so, how is one to respond to threats short of total war but still deemed serious? How does one go about defending and fighting back without going truly nuclear — that is, going to nuclear war?

In the 1950s, this dilemma was one of credibility. The massive retaliation policy rested precariously on the belief that the United States would be prepared and willing to sacrifice New York for Paris or London in a nuclear exchange with the Soviets. Today, the dilemma is one of nuclear temptation as a default. In the absence of an independent nuclear capability, and in the face of a nuclear North Korea, South Korea or Japan may feel the acute need to respond to nuclear threats by North Korea without going nuclear itself. A diplomatic and military panacea may be the sharing of some missile defense technologies and platforms. The continuation of a U.S. nuclear umbrella and the establishment of a missile defense system are not mutually exclusive. Both can be had — without the attending "arms race" that some portend. In East Asia, both are needed.

At a force deployment level, the United States can reconfigure its command structure in Korea as well as update its arsenal. Currently, the arsenal inventory of U.S. missile forces in Korea is comprised mostly of MK-84s leftover from Vietnam. Putting Joint Direct Attack Munition (JDAM) kits on them would neatly make smart these dumb bombs, making virtue out of necessity.

Currently, the commander in Korea wears three hats. The 4-star general who commands Korea is Commander in Chief, UN Command (CINCUNC), Commander, Combined Forces Command (CFC), and Commander, USFK. The army component of USFK is the commander of the Eighth U.S. Army.

To be sure, such command structure reflects the historically international nature of the situation on the Korean peninsula, but it also reflects the complex bilateral relationship with South Korea. Given recent political developments in South Korea, as well as our rethinking of our own "footprint" in East Asia and the reconfiguration of our overall worldwide deployment, we may want to explore the possibility of consolidating the command structure in Korea and Japan with a North East Asian command based in Guam. We can explore the idea of returning to a subregional commander within Pacific Command (PACOM) such as a Commander in Chief, North East Asia (CINCNEA), similar to a Commander in Chief, Far East (CINCFE) that we had in the 1940s and 1950s.

An important step is to redefine the "language" of proliferation, its symbols and syntax. We need a defining doctrine in the tradition of the Monroe Doctrine and NSC-68 to confront this problem. Every doctrine has its key words and grammar. The new doctrine's vocabulary should be "prevention." Its new grammar should be new targeting guidelines. The White House's new Office of Global Communications should propagate U.S. values on nuclear proliferation. After all, our values on nuclear proliferation are just as important as the rule of law, freedom of speech, private property, religious tolerance, and equal justice.

Operation IRAQI FREEDOM may be a threshold in military operations. Deterrence, containment, and preemption have to a certain degree been part of U.S. policy. But going after leadership targets in the very beginning of war is a big shift in thinking. It has rendered ineffective the thrust of effects-based operations, to wit, that punishing the ruled will pressure the ruler to sue for peace. As President Bush said: "With new tactics and precision weapons, we can achieve military objectives without directing violence against civilians. No device of man removes the tragedy from war; yet it is a great moral advance when the guilty have far more to fear from war than the innocent."[47] Nothing symbolizes more eloquently and delivers a more powerful message than this new targeting philosophy.

If one were to deduce the logical corollary of this shift in thinking, one can propose that the United States expand on the recent National

Strategy on WMD: "The United States will continue to make clear that it reserves the right to respond with overwhelming force — including resort to all of our options — to the use of WMD against the United States, our forces abroad, and friends and allies."[48] This clause can be expanded to include those regimes that give materials to terrorists that could be used to make WMD. The implicit threat of nuclear annihilation for giving sensitive nuclear materials to terrorists should be contemplated as the ultimate deterrent option. North Korea must be made to understand clearly that the pain and cost of selling sensitive nuclear materials to terrorists are that it must then live under a serious and credible nuclear threat.

Lastly, as important as changes in organizational structure, deployments, and language may be, they pale in comparison to the role of individual personalities. The insouciance of sophisticated theories of international relations has yet to successfully traduce the age-old importance of individuals. Personalities matter a great deal even as predicting the rise of key players in China, Japan, and the two Koreas is extremely difficult. One may be unduly optimistic in expecting the emergence of an East Asian trio of Metternich, Castlereagh, and Talleyrand, and an East Asian Congress equivalent of that of 1815 Vienna. But the difficulty of prediction and the disappointment of high expectations should not preclude the United States from seeking to identify and investigate key players, and their intellectual and social backgrounds.

For example, a North Korea without Kim Jong Il, but one still with nuclear weapons and a sub-par human rights record, is certainly far from ideal. One cannot state with certainty that a North Korean military figure or one of Kim's sons or relatives will not be as cruel and totalitarian as Kim Jong Il. But I posit that it is still preferable to one with Kim at the helm. The stability of the status quo, as advocated by "realists" is misguided. The status quo itself is inherently unstable. Realistic solutions posed by the realists have produced little in the way of stability or realism. Regime change in North Korea will be destabilizing. But the uncertainty of a future without Kim Jong Il should not hamper our intellectual exploration and policy execution of a North Korea state in the absence of a Kim regime.

Some 20 years elapsed between the signing of the Versailles Treaty and the Munich agreement. We cannot emulate that historical pattern. It is conceivable and desirable that 20 years after the North Korean withdrawal from the NPT, a new nonproliferation set-up, based on a strengthening of our existing bilateral alliances and the establishing of a new understanding with China, will guide the United States and East Asian nations in the second decade of the 21st century. Disraeli said, "Man is not a creature of circumstances. Circumstances are the creatures of men." The year 2025 in East Asia need not be an *Annus Horribilis*. The United States must and will shape our circumstances as it fits our needs.

CHAPTER 1 - ENDNOTES

1. "The National Security Strategy of the United States of America," September 17, 2002, *www.whitehouse.gov*.

2. For a horrific fantasy, see Paul Johnson, "There Arose Out of the Pits the Smoke of a Great Furnace," *The Spectator*, December 7, 2002.

3. Press accounts relish this notion. For recent examples, see John Larkin and Donald Macintyre, "Your Move, Mr. Kim," *Time*, September 1, 2003; Peter Landesman, "Arms and the Man," *New York Times Magazine*, August 17, 2003; Jack Kelly, "Brinksmanship Bartering," *Washington Times*, September 3, 2003.

4. *People's Daily*, November 7, 2003.

5. "India Starts to See China as a Land of Business Opportunity," *Financial Times*, September 23, 2003.

6. For different scenarios, see Hideshi Takesada, "A Unified Korean Peninsula: Five Scenarios and the Significance of Japan-US Cooperation," *http://www. glocomnet.or.jp*.

7. Similar to the initiation of the debate over *sonderweg* in Germany in 1999 during Kosovo, discussions about Japan's "normalcy" have begun in light of the North Korean threat. Howard French, "Japan Faces Burden: Its Own Defense," *New York Times*, July 22, 2003.

8. "Japan Nuclear Deterrent Idea Hit," *The Japan Times*, August 7, 2003.

9. Interview, Dr. Jeong Jong-Ho, Professor of Chinese Studies, Seoul National University, July 2, 2003, Seoul, Korea. For the "spread" of Chinese influence, see Peter Baker, "A Tense Divide in Russia's Far East," *Washington Post*, July 29, 2003.

10. "Chinese in Belgrade, Beijing Protest NATO Embassy Bombing," May 9, 1999, *http://www.cnn.com*.

11. "China's First Astronaut Crowned 'Space Hero,'" *People's Daily*, November 7, 2003.

12. John Hill, "China's Armed Forces Set to Undergo Face-Lift," *Jane's Intelligence Review*, February 2003, pp. 10-15.

13. "Former JDA Head, LDP Officials' Roundup on Nuclear Arms," *Tokyo Sapio*, June 11, 2003, *Foreign Broadcast Information Service* (FBIS): JPP20030702000049. Former JDA Chief Gen Nakatani, Senior Vice Minister of the Cabinet Office, LDP Security Policy Diet League Chairman Kenzo Yoneda, and LDP Director of National Defense Division Yasukazu Hamada participated in the discussion.

14. "Abe, Yoneda on DPRK, Defense, Japan-US Alliance," *Tokyo Seiron*, September 2003, FBIS: JPP20030808000050. Yoneda is senior vice-minister of the Cabinet Office.

15. "Junior Lawmakers' Group Urgently Calls for Security Measures," *Tokyo Sekai Shuho*, FBIS: JPP20030813000048, August 19-26, 2003. See also Yoshio Okubo, "Time to Overhaul National Defense Program," *Daily Yomiuri*, August 7, 2003.

16. Abe's father was Shintaro Abe, former secretary-general of the LDP, and his grandfather was former Prime Minister Nobusuke Kishi. Abe recently became LDP secretary-general at the age of 49. Abe is a strong candidate to replace Koizumi as Prime Minister.

17. *Chosun Ilbo*, October 23, 2003; *Daily Yomiuri*, November 3, 2003.

18. Interview with a North Korean soldier defector, "Kim Jong Il's Army Diverts all Aid to Itself," *Wolgan Chosun*, October 2003.

19. "To Become Strong is the Only Option," *Tehran Jomhuri-ye Eslami*, FBIS: IAP20030914000027, September 13, 2003.

20. Henry Sokolski, "Contending with a Nuclear-Armed North Korea," *Joint Force Quarterly*, Autumn 2002.

21. Robert Walpole, "North Korea's Taepo Dong Launch and Some Implications on the Ballistic Missile Threat to the United States," December 8, 1998, Central Intelligence Agency, *http://www.cia.gov*.

22. The "386" generation label euphemistically refers to those who were the "democracy movement" generation. To be sure, there are those who did not participate in the myriad student demonstrations of the 1980s. Moreover, due to a 3-year compulsory military service, some 386ers are in their forties.

23. For a sociological survey, see Chae-Han Kim, "Who in South Korea Trust North Korea and Who Trust the United States?" *The Korean Journal of Defense Analysis*, Fall 2002.

24. *Jusapa* is a radical faction of the student movement that lionizes and takes guidance from Kim Il Sung's *Juche* ideology.

25. For qualified optimism on the engagement policy and North Korea, see Choo-Suk Suh, "North Korea's 'Military-First' Policy and Inter-Korean Relations," *The Korean Journal of Defense Analysis*, Fall 2002.

26. For Choe's speech, see *http://www.hannara.or.kr*, June 26, 2003. For the intra-party friction, see *http://www.ohmynews.com*, September 2, 2003; and *http://www.independent.co.kr*, September 11, 2003.

27. "The Cost of Self-Reliance," *Chosun Ilbo*, September 3, 2003.

28. *Joongang Ilbo*, September 25, 2003.

29. *Chosun Ilbo*, November 4, 2003.

30. South Korea's first president, Syngman Rhee, was the first statesman to raise the idea of a "Pacific Pact" or what he termed, "Alliance Mutual Security." But Rhee envisioned a "PATO" that excluded Japan, composed only of the Republics of Korea, China, Vietnam, the Philippines, Hong Kong, Macao, and Thailand. See author, *Master of Manipulation: Syngman Rhee and the Seoul-Washington Alliance, 1953-1960*, Seoul: Yonsei University Press, 2001, p.173n.

31. *Ashai Shimbun*, November 6, 2003.

32. "Japan Signals Shift on $2bn Tehran Oil Deal," *Financial Times*, September 25, 2003.

33. "U.S. troop Strength in Korea Can Be Cut, Pace Says," October 10, 2003, *www.nyjt.com*.

34. "5 Nations Confirmed to Security Council," *Washington Times*, October 24, 2003.

35. Tyler Cowen, "The Game Theory of Nuclear Proliferation," September 25, 2003, *www2.techcentralstation.com*.

36. Doug Bandow, "Ending the Anachronistic Korean Commitment," *Parameters*, Summer 2003, pp. 78-88.

37. Thomas B. Fargo, "Operationalizing the Asia-Pacific Defense Strategy," *Joint Force Quarterly*, Autumn 2002.

38. See Joseph Cirincione, "The Asian Nuclear Reaction Chain," March 2000, *http://www.ceip.org*; Sokolski, *op.cit*. For Chinese MIRV capability, see John Hill, "China Modernises Missile Force," *Jane's Intelligence Review*, March 1, 2003.

39. On the various futures for Korea, see Nicholas Eberstadt, "Alternative Scenarios for the Korean Peninsula," *Strategic Asia 2004-05*, pp. 109-137.

40. In 1994 nearly every Western observer got it wrong. A succession was impossible, they argued, highlighting Kim Jong Il's playboy lifestyle, playing up Oh Jinwoo's credentials as Defense Minister and confidant of Kim Il Sung, and Kim Pyong Il's good looks, charisma, and leadership skills.

41. For this view, see Kim Sung-Han, quoted in *Joongang Ilbo*, February 27, 2003.

42. For a representative sample, see Victor Cha, "Defensive Realism and Japan's Approach toward Korean Reunification," *The National Bureau of Asian Research*, Vol. 14, No. 1, June 2003, pp. 5-32. See also, Hideshi Takesada, "A Unified Korean Peninsula," *op.cit*.

43. For a somber analysis, see Arun Sahgal, "China in Space: Military Implications," *Asia Times*, November 5, 2003. For a provocative article, see "China Preparing Space War against U.S.," October 30, 2003, *www.newsmax.com*.

44. Susan V. Lawrence, "Dueling over Sanctions," *Far Eastern Economic Review*, November 6, 2003.

45. Gordon Thompson, "Treaty a Useful Relic," *Bulletin of the Atomic Scientists*, July/August 1990.

46. Mohamed ElBaradei recently proposed a Baruch Plan for the 21st century, advocating "multinational control" over access to highly enriched uranium and plutonium. "U.N. Nuke Chief Seeks Stringent Controls," *Washington Times*, November 3, 2003.

47. "Let Tyrants Fear," President Bush's speech aboard the *U.S.S. Lincoln*, May 5, 2003, *www.whitehouse.gov*.

48. National Strategy to Combat Weapons of Mass Destruction, December 2002, *www.whitehouse.gov*.

CHAPTER 2

PROLIFERATION IN THE MIDDLE EAST:
WHO IS NEXT AFTER IRAN?

Patrick Clawson

Were Iran to acquire nuclear weapons, its neighbors and the entire region would have to consider carefully the impact on their own security situation. The sobering reality is that several other Middle Eastern countries would seriously consider acquiring nuclear weapons were Iran to do so. Indeed, there could be a vicious cycle in which first one additional country acquires nuclear weapons, then others concerned about that country's possession proceed with their own weapons programs, and that further proliferation in turn convinces more countries to act.

The thesis of this chapter is that such a proliferation outbreak is distinctly possible unless the United States responds to Iranian proliferation with firm, concrete measures to offset Iran's actions.[1] The structure of the chapter is to briefly summarize the reasons for concern about the Iranian nuclear program and then to turn to the potential proliferants: Saudi Arabia, Egypt, other Arab states, and Turkey. The chapter closes with what the United States could do to influence the decisions of Middle East states about whether or not to imitate an Iranian proliferation.

Reasons to Worry about the Iranian Nuclear Program.

Repeated warnings by U.S. officials about a potential Iranian nuclear weapon have been regarded as exaggerated by many academic students of Iran. The mid-1990s warnings that Iran might have a nuclear weapon within 5 years turned out to be overly pessimistic. But it appears that after years of problems and delays, Iran's nuclear ambitions have made considerable progress. The March 2003 visit by a United Nations (UN) International Atomic Energy Agency (IAEA) team showed that Iran was well along on its announced commitment to developing a full fuel cycle capability. Iran has aknowledged to the IAEA that it is constructing a plan to convert natural uranium, which Iran is mining from domestic deposits, into uranium hexafluoride gas. That gas presumably would be used in the Nantanz enrichment facility visited by the IAEA team. The Nantanz facility has 160 functioning centrifuges in a pilot facility, while 1,000 more centrifuges are being assembled in another building which is planned to hold 5,000 centrifuges.[2] While Nantanz could be used to produce lightly enriched uranium to refuel the electrical power generating reactor under construction at Bushehr, it also would be capable of producing highly enriched uranium. Depending on the capacity of the machines, the facility when completed in 2005 could produce enough highly enriched uranium for two or more nuclear bombs per year.

Meanwhile, satellite photos indicate Iran also is building a heavy water production plant which raises troubling concerns, given that Iran is not known to have a reactor that would make use of the plant's production and such a reactor could well be a means to acquire plutonium, giving Iran a second route to a nuclear weapon. And construction on the light-water reactor at Bushehr is making substantial headway, with commissioning of the plant likely in 2004, which means that Iran will shortly thereafter accumulate spent fuel in holding tanks. The fuel will be too radioactive to be returned immediately to Russia, even assuming that the long-discussed agreement to return the fuel is made operative. If heroic efforts are made to return the spent fuel to Russia while still quite hot, the spent fuel in the holding tanks will provide Iran the material from which it could extract highly fissile material for several dozen weapons in relatively short order. In short, considering the progress it is making on several different facilities, it seems accurate to say that Iran is developing a substantial nuclear infrastructure.

Of course, it is possible that Iran will use this nuclear infrastructure only for the announced goal of a self-sufficient nuclear power industry rather than for pursuing nuclear weapons. However, four factors suggest Iran will perceive that the constraints against proliferation are not great compared to the reasons to acquire nuclear weapons.

1. *Attitude Towards Arms Control Agreements.* Iran is a state-party to the Treaty on the Nonproliferation of Nuclear Weapons (NPT), but that may not constrain its nuclear program. Iran's attitude towards

arms control agreements is not reassuring. Iran's declaration to the Organization for the Prevention of Chemical Weapons (OPCW) pursuant to the Chemical Weapons Convention (CWC) denied that Iran had ever produced chemical weapons, which is a transparent lie. U.S. sources say Iran imported uranium hexaflouride from China without declaring this to the IAEA, and that some of this has been enriched, which would violate its NPT obligations. Meanwhile, Iran has refused to accept the enhanced IAEA inspections under the Program 93+2 Additional Protocol; indeed, it has not modified its safeguard agreement with the IAEA to incorporate the IAEA's 1995 restatement of what it is empowered to do with its powers to enforce the NPT. (This restatement was the first part of the two-part Program 93+2, with the Additional Protocol). Nor is Iran going beyond the minimum required under its current safeguard agreement, as evidenced by its recent delays in notifying the IAEA about the construction of new facilities (about which the IAEA was well aware because of satellite photos), and its refusal to allow inspection of those facilities (as distinct from a walk-through "visit" without any examination of the facility by experts). All of this despite the European Union (EU) pressure for progress about nuclear transparency before Iran can get the trade agreement with the EU it badly wants.

It would be fair to characterize Iran's attitude towards the NPT as doing the minimum required while loudly proclaiming its adherence. That is discouraging for the hopes of using the NPT to constrain Iran's nuclear program, because as interpreted by the IAEA, the NPT gives Iran every right to build robust uranium enrichment and plutonium extraction capabilities if it declares those activities, while simultaneously developing the expertise and equipment to weaponize the fissile material; that is, the IAEA view is that only assembling the fissile material into weapons is prohibited. And the NPT gives Iran the right to withdraw with 6 months' notice. So Iran could remain in good standing with the IAEA even as it acquired the capability for a rapid breakout once leaving the NPT, that is, for developing dozens of bombs within a short period. This route would allow Iran to claim adherence to the NPT while still having a nuclear potential so obvious and awesome as to worry, if not intimidate, neighboring countries.

2. *International Reaction to Proliferation.* The contrast between how the world — especially, but not only the United States — reacts to Iraq and to North Korea could have troubling implications for Iranian proliferation. The correct lesson which Iran should draw from the contract is the advantages accruing to those who offer to negotiate with the United States and proclaim their willingness to make strategic compromises if offered the right incentives, compared to the high price paid by those who refuse to cooperate. But Iran may well draw from the contrast the wrong lesson, namely, that those who have nuclear weapons are treated with kid gloves, while those who do not are treated with boxing gloves. In other words, Iran may conclude that the best, if not the only, way to deter the United States is to possess nuclear weapons. And there is the possibility that a defiant, nuclear North Korea might aid proliferation in Iran. Respected Israeli military analyst Ze'ev Schiff warns, "Israel fears that if the North Korean crisis is not settled, Pyongyang would try to form an anti-American coalition in the Middle East comprising Iran, Syria, and Libya."[3]

3. *Threat Environment.* The overthrow of Saddam Hussein greatly reduces the threat of invasion from Iraq; it is difficult to see why — or for that matter, how — a new Iraqi government would want to invade Iran. And the end of the Saddam regime could well lead over time to a reduced U.S. presence in the Gulf — a presence which Tehran has often complained is aimed at it rather than Baghdad. Plus, Kuwait and Saudi Arabia are likely, post-Saddam, to cut their military spending; indeed, all the Arab monarchies of the Gulf are facing economic and social pressures which make large weapons purchases less attractive. Just as the threat from the Gulf is on the decline, so, too, the potential for an Iranian-Israeli confrontation fades if Hezbollah is reined in by Syria, which is distinctly possible given Syrian concerns about U.S. pressure after the overthrow of Saddam. But unfortunately, there is little reason to expect that the reduction in regional threats will change Iran's determination to acquire nuclear weapons. The perceived threat from the United States will remain; indeed, it could become more preoccupying, if Iran's leaders worry that Washington may be tempted to promote overthrow of the Islamic Republic by the increasingly disaffected youth. Since, as discussed above, deterrence of the United States could be seen by Iranian leaders to require

nuclear weapons, the perceived greater U.S. threat would increase the motivation to acquire nuclear weapons.

Domestic Political Environment.

Iran's domestic political scene is characterized by a bitter dispute between hardliners and reformers. But there is little evidence that the two camps differ in their approach to nuclear weapons. Being better informed about the outside world, the reformers may be more sensitive to the political price Iran would pay for proliferation. On the other hand, the reformers are more nationalist; indeed, they have at times criticized hardliners for putting ideological regime interests above national interests. It would seem that the opposition, which has blocked Majlis ratification of the Comprehensive Test Ban Treaty (CTBT), came more from reformers than from hardliners. It seems that both hardliners and reformers see Iran as strategically isolated, unable to rely for its security on allies or on foreign weapons suppliers. The argument goes that Iran must therefore develop indigenous weapons capabilities. But the prospects are poor that Iran could develop on its own world-class conventional arms, despite the billions of dollars it is spending to develop a full range of conventional weapons systems. Convinced of this analysis, dedicated Iranian nationalists, no matter how democratic or desirous of good relations with America, may indeed support Iran pursuing nuclear weapons. In his February 18, 2003, testimony to the Senate Intelligence Committee, Central Intelligence Agency (CIA) Director George Tenet stated, "No Iranian government, regardless of its ideological leanings, is likely to willingly abandon WMD [weapons of mass destruction] programs that are seen as guaranteeing Iran's security."

Faced with Iranian nuclear progress and the limited prospects that international or domestic factors will lead Iran to back off from the pursuit of nuclear weapons, it would be quite appropriate for Middle Eastern countries to consider the security implications were Iran to acquire nuclear weapons. It would not be surprising if some countries were already developing their contingency plans. This chapter asks, what are the prospect those plans could include acquisition of nuclear weapons?

Saudi Arabia: Proliferation Consistent with the NPT.

Saudi Arabia is the state most likely to proliferate in response to an Iranian nuclear threat. To be sure, such an action could threaten the U.S.-Saudi relationship which has been the foundation of Saudi security. But the Saudis keenly remember that when they felt threatened by Iran — in the early days of the revolution, when the Iran-Iraq war was starting — the U.S. response to their entreaties was to send to the Gulf F-15 fighters which President Jimmy Carter publicly described as being unarmed. As Richard Russell put it, "It would be imprudent, to say the least, for Riyadh to make the cornerstone of their national-security posture out of an assumption that the United States would come to the kingdom's defense — under any and all circumstances."[4]

A nuclear-armed Iran could well see itself as the natural leader of the region to which all other states should listen closely. That would fit with the Iranian nationalist self-conception, which sees Iran as a great and ancient civilization in contrast to the parvenu unsophisticates in the Arab minor statelets of the Gulf (that is a toned-down version of comments Iranian nationalists make about their neighbors in the Arab Gulf monarchies). Saudi Arabia would have excellent reason to worry about Iran projecting itself as the protector of the Saudi Shia community and as a state which should be consulted about how to manage the Mecca pilgrimage and holy sites — all of which would be utterly unacceptable to Riyadh.

Saudi Arabia might be unsure how much assistance it could count on from the United States in face of such Iranian indirect intimidation, which might not rise to the level at which Washington would be prepared to risk a crisis with Iran. Riyadh may therefore deem it necessary to possess a self-defense capability against Iranian intimidation. And Saudi Arabia is in no position to defend itself with conventional means, as is well illustrated by how ineffective the Saudi military remains despite spending billions of dollars each year on the most advanced weaponry and on training by U.S. advisors. So a nuclear option could fit with the Saudi needs.

An instructive case to consider is the Saudi 1986 acquisition of 50-60 CSS-2 missiles and 10-15 mobile launchers from China — missiles used by China for its nuclear forces which can carry a warhead of up to 2,500 kg to a range of 700 km.[5] While the Saudis and the Chinese both insist that the warheads are conventional, the missiles are a peculiar way to deliver conventional explosives, since they are highly inaccurate (with a circular error of probability of about 1-2 km). The Saudis acquired the missiles without detection by the United States, and they since steadily have refused to allow any outside inspections of the missiles—suggesting that the Saudis have both the capability and the willingness to acquire advanced weapons in the face of strong U.S. objections.

The CSS-2s raise an interesting question. There is a widespread impression in West and South Asia that Saudi Arabia provided much of the finance for the Pakistani nuclear program in return for a rumored Pakistani commitment to provide Saudi Arabia nuclear warheads if needed. Pakistan has been interested in developing nuclear warheads for its missiles. Richard Russell speculates, "The Saudis might be willing to help fund Pakistani research, development, and deployment costs for their nuclear-tipped ballistic missiles in exchange for nuclear warheads."[6] It would be possible to structure such an arrangement without violating Saudi obligations under the NPT. As explained to this writer by a senior Pakistani official well versed in the matter, Pakistan and Saudi Arabia could follow the example set by the United States and Germany during the Cold War with dual-key missiles. America and Germany took the position that Germany was not violating the NPT when the United States stored nuclear warheads under its control in Germany even though the delivery means for those warheads were missiles under German control. So Pakistan could store in Saudi Arabia nuclear warheads designed to fit on to Saudi-controlled missiles.

Egypt: Proliferation to Maintain Its Status.

Were Iran to acquire nuclear weapons, that would affect the on-going debate in Egypt about whether it needs to nuclearize to maintain its status as a regional power. If, in addition, Saudi Arabia were to acquire nuclear weapons—even if by the indirect Pakistani route described above—it is difficult to see Egypt remaining non-nuclear, because it would be unacceptable to Egypt to be perceived as a less potent power than another Arab country.

What would drive Egyptian decisions about proliferation would be its determination to be the leading Arab power. There is broad consensus among the Egyptian elite that such a status requires that Egypt have the most powerful Arab army: the Egyptian view is that great states have great armies. It is worth recalling that the original Egyptian proposal for a WMD-free zone in the Middle East came after Iraqi president Saddam Hussein threatened in 1990 to "burn half of Israel." Perhaps Egypt's motivation was to protect Israel, but certainly one could argue for the alternative interpretation that Egypt could not accept another Arab state having a more potent WMD capability than Egypt possessed. Indeed, the 1998 Indian and Pakistani nuclear tests led to a debate in Egypt about proliferation, with Egyptian President Hosny Mubarak suggesting that these could lead to a generalized proliferation throughout the region.

An obvious factor in the Egyptian calculus about proliferation is Israel. The WMD imbalance with Israel is a deep wound. Egypt is bitter that it has had no success in securing an Israeli commitment to give up nuclear weapons within a fixed time frame. Israel has offered that 2 years after it has peace treaties with all regional states, it would begin negotiations on a robust regional inspection process which once functional would monitor Israeli denuclearization. Faced with the perceived imbalance, Egypt has long had a strong pro-nuclear lobby. Egyptian president Hosny Mubarak stated in 1998, "when the time comes and we need nuclear weapons, we will not hesitate." In May 2002, former Egyptian representative to the IAEA Dr. Mustafa al-Fiqi wrote an article for the semi-official *Alhram* newspaper questioning whether President Anwar Sadat made the right decision when he suddenly and surprisingly signed the NPT in 1981; al-Fiqi argued that nuclear weapons might have been a useful deterrent against Israel.[7]

It is also worth noting that Egypt has long had an ambiguous attitude about WMD. Egypt has refused to sign the Chemical Weapons Convention. It has a history of using chemical weapons in 1964 in its war in Yemen—at the time, documented by the International Committee of the Red Cross and discussed in the Security Council. So there is no taboo in Egyptian thinking about the use of WMD.

Other Arab States: Those with Ambitions Lack Capability.

Other Arab states would not pose as much a proliferation worry. Those that could proliferate would not particularly want to; those that would want to would have a hard time doing so.

Syria would be very unlikely to change its approach to nuclear weapons in the event of an Iranian nuclear acquisition. Syrian weapons decisions are not driven by prestige factors, in part because Syria does not see itself as the natural leader of the Arab world. And Syria is quite aware of how severely Israel would react to a Syrian nuclear acquisition. Syria has been quite clear-headed in thinking through its WMD options. It has been bent for more than a decade on acquiring a large enough inventory of CW-tipped missiles that it can threaten Israel with unacceptable losses. And Syria has been relatively responsible about its CW-tipped missiles, giving every indication that it sees these as weapons of last resort to be used only if Israel threatened Syria's national existence. Given the strategic logic to this approach—it is after all reasonable for Syria to worry about the country being overrun and to therefore have a weapon of last resort—it is not surprising that the U.S. response to the Syrian CW proliferation effort has been rather low-key. So much for the charge that the U.S. government has a dual standard about the Israeli nuclear program: in fact, Washington has been rather understanding when Middle East states faced with existential threats acquire a WMD capability appropriate to that threat. Indeed, it is remarkable that the United States has done so little about the Syrian WMD threat, given the bad relations between the two countries and the fact that Syria's WMD threatens a close U.S. ally, namely, Israel.

In the category of countries that would want to proliferate but would have problems doing so, the most obvious case before Qadafi's nuclear renunciation, was Libya. The Palestinians might try to proliferate—after all, most of them think they are already being attacked with WMD (i.e., chemical and biological weapons) by Israel—but they have a low capability to buy or build nuclear weapons. Of greater proliferation worry would be the smaller Gulf Cooperation Council (GCC) states, especially the United Arab Emirates, which are well-placed to buy nuclear weapons if anyone can, but it is not at all clear that there would be anyone prepared to sell such weapons.

Turkey: Will NATO Be Enough?

Historically Turkey has been at peace with Iran, and the two countries have generally paid relatively little attention to each other, compared to what one might expect from two neighbors with considerable economic interaction. That said, Turkey has many reasons to worry about meddling by an Islamic Republic which is ideologically opposed to Ankara's secular policies. If Turkey faces serious internal problems — be it from Islamists or from Kurds — Iran might seek to take advantage of that situation, and Iranian nuclear weapons would make Turkey think long and hard about how much it could complain about such Iranian meddling. In other words, an Iranian nuclear capability could make the Turkish General Staff nervous.

Faced with a nuclear-armed Iran, Turkey's first instinct would be to turn to the North Atlantic Treaty Organization (NATO). Turkey places extraordinary value on its NATO membership, which symbolizes the West's acceptance of Turkey — a delicate issue for a country which feels it is excluded from the EU on civilizational grounds more than for any other reason. The cold reality is that NATO was not designed to defend Turkey: assisting Turkey faced with a general Warsaw Pact invasion of Western Europe is one thing; defending Turkey when it alone faces a threat is an altogether different matter. It is not clear how much NATO members want to take on this burden. It will be only natural for Turkey to wonder how much it can rely on NATO.

Were Turkey to decide that it had to proliferate in order to defend itself, it has good industrial and scientific infrastructures which it could draw upon to build nuclear weapons on its own. It would be difficult to prevent a determined Turkey from building nuclear weapons in well under a decade.

How Can America Influence Middle East Decisions after Iranian Proliferation?

Whether or not Iranian acquisition of nuclear weapons leads to further proliferation among America's friends in the region will depend in considerable part on what policies the United States adopts as Iran's nuclear capabilities become more evident. Were Washington to do little besides deploring Iran's actions, further proliferation is likely. That is the case irrespective of how loudly and frequently the United States condemns Iran's actions.

Calls for economic sanctions or diplomatic steps against Iran seem an unpromising way to affect the calculus of other proliferants. For one thing, it is not clear that the international community would agree to impose sanctions. For more than a decade, the United States and the EU nations have profoundly disagreed about the utility of sanctions on Iran, and attitudes have hardened on both sides. It is hard to see the EU abandoning its long-held opposition to sanctions, since it is firmly convinced that engagement is the best way to moderate Iranian policy and to support Iranian moderates. Furthermore, it is not clear how much impact sanctions would have on Iranian actions; the impact of the long-standing unilateral U.S. sanctions is subject to different readings. All in all, other regional states pondering proliferation would probably be skeptical that sanctions would change Iran's policy, and they might not even been greatly concerned that they would face sanctions were they to proliferate.

Nor is it clear how much impact there would be if the United States responded by reemphasizing controls on exports of sensitive technology. Such export controls would seem unlikely to influence Iranian actions, since Iran has in theory faced strict controls for some time and yet has managed to make do, one way or another. The impact of reinvigorated export controls on the proliferation plans of the regional states would vary. A country like Turkey, which might consider building its own weapons, would presumably be more vulnerable, whereas countries that might consider acquiring nuclear weapons fully assembled, such as the Gulf monarchies, would presumably be less affected.

In the event of Iranian acquisition of nuclear weapons, the most promising U.S. anti-proliferation tool would be closer security ties with allies threatened by the Iranian proliferation breakthrough. America's friends in the region are going to feel more vulnerable in the face of Iranian nuclear weapons, and they will need to be reassured that their security concerns are being met if they are to

37

be dissuaded from imitating Iran's proliferation. The United States could reassure them through some combination of policies that:

- Change declaratory posture. For instance, were the United States explicitly to extend a nuclear umbrella over its regional friends, that could weigh heavily in the minds of regional leaders—especially if done loudly, frequently, and at the highest levels.

- Enhance access to advanced weapons. For instance, if the United States assisted regional states in acquiring improved missile/air defenses that could lessen the threat posed by Iranian nuclear-tipped missiles.

- Expand U.S. presence in the region. To take an extreme example, if the United States were to station ships with nuclear-capable cruise missiles off Iran's shores, that would make a powerful point about the depth of U.S. commitment to the changed declaratory posture cited above.

These policies to reassure U.S. friends in the region would have the added advantage of showing that Iran's security has become worse off because of its acquisition of nuclear weapons—that is, Iran's nuclear weapons would have increased the U.S. military threat to Iran, rather than providing a means to balance the greater power of the United States. That would be a useful precedent for other regional actors to contemplate in that it would suggest that the acquisition of nuclear weapons, in fact, may not be a force-enhancer. If the United States can point to strong actions it has taken to counter Iranian nuclear weapons, that will lend more credibility to U.S. warnings to its friends in the region that were they to proliferate, Washington might take the strong step of reducing or ending the U.S. security relationship with their country. This could become a significant factor in their calculations about whether to head down the proliferation path.

ENDNOTES - CHAPTER 2

1. This chapter was originally presented before a dinner seminar of the Nonproliferation Policy Education Center, Washington, DC, April 2003.

2. Joby Warrick and Glenn Kessler, "Iran's Nuclear Program Speeds Ahead," *The Washington Post*, March 10, 2003, pp. A1 and A17.

3. Ze'ev Schiff, "Weapons of Mass Destruction and the Middle East: The View from Israel," monograph from James A. Baker III Institute for Public Policy at Rice University, March 2003.

4. Richard Russell, "A Saudi Nuclear Option?," *Survival*, Vol. 43, No. 2, Summer 2001, p. 70.

5. Anthony Cordesman, *Saudi Arabia: Guarding the Desert Kingdom*, Boulder: Westview Press, 1997, p. 178.

6. Russell, p. 75.

7. Cited in Emily Landau, "Egypt's Nuclear Dilemma," *Strategic Assessment* (from the Tel Aviv University Jaffee Center for Strategic Studies), Vol. 5, No. 3, November 2002, p. 26.

CHAPTER 3

NUCLEAR 1914: THE NEXT BIG WORRY

Henry D. Sokolski

The next use of nuclear weapons, if followed quickly by others, is nothing the United States or its closest friends could suffer lightly. Like Rome after it was repeatedly pillaged, Washington, even if not directly attacked, would find its authority immediately undermined. Powerless to stop nuclear attacks after having so long warned against them, the United States could soon find itself under assault. Assuming nuclear use begets nuclear use, what would follow could be the next dark ages.

An alternative and sunnier future would be one in which the United States and its allies can and do limit severely the use of nuclear weapons. The question is: What would this require? At a minimum, enough nations falling into line, either voluntarily or otherwise, to keep nuclear attacks at bay.

This is hardly a sure thing. Most nuclear-capable states are reluctant to provide information on their nuclear inventories, activities, and facilities, which is necessary to check nuclear proliferation or terrorism. As more states acquire nuclear weapons or become increasingly ready to do so, the inclination to share such facts is only likely to decline. Nuclear-capable states are unlikely to open up if it implicates them in proliferation or undermines their option to acquire nuclear weapons in the future.

The news since September 11, 2001, is depressingly instructive in this regard. More than a year after the first revelations about Iran's uranium enrichment program were made public, the United States and the International Atomic Energy Agency (IAEA) were still trying to drag information about A. Q. Khan's nuclear activities from the Pakistani government. First, Islamabad denied that any Pakistani ever shared nuclear technology with anyone. Then, after Iranian officials fingered Pakistan, the Pakistani government admitted that Dr. Khan had made some sales to Tehran. Then it was revealed that

Dr. Khan and his subordinates sold plans, equipment, and bomb designs to Libya. Pakistani President Pervez Musharraf had Dr. Khan arrested — but just as suddenly decided to grant the Pakistani scientist a pardon, praising him as a national hero. The United States and the IAEA are still anxiously trying to learn what exactly Dr. Khan sold and to whom. But so far, the Pakistani government has refused to allow either the United States or the IAEA to interview Dr. Khan directly.

It is not just Iran and Libya that benefited from Pakistani nuclear exports. Several other countries, including North Korea, Egypt, and perhaps even Brazil have received them as well. Brazil's case is unclear because its navy has put off allowing inspectors full access to the country's enrichment plant for nearly a year, for fear that IAEA officials might pinpoint the foreign sources of their imported enrichment equipment. Pakistan could be of immense help in this situation. But so far, it has done the bare minimum to clarify matters. How successful might we be, then, in securing nuclear materials and facilities against terrorist theft or in tracking down nuclear terrorists in a world with more Pakistans and Brazils? If the past year of news is prologue, our prospects do not look good.

An Unsteady Balance.

More speculative but every bit as chilling is how such nations might use their own nuclear capabilities against one another. Here, too, there is cause to worry. A key reason why is the amount of diplomatic entropy since the collapse of the Soviet Union. During the Cold War, there was a clear subordination of nations to one or another of the two superpowers' strong alliance systems. More important, the aim of the alliance in the West was to check or contain the efforts of the Warsaw Pact. The net effect was relative peace with only small wars (see Figure 1).

This system no longer exists. Instead, we now have one superpower, the United States, with a growing but relatively weak alliance system being challenged by an increasing number of nuclear or nuclear-weapons-ready states. So far, the United States has tried to cope with the emergence of these independent nuclear powers by making them "strategic partners," e.g., India and Russia, or "non-

Cold War
1945-1990

Strong Containment
1 Critical Strategic Military Balance

Figure 1.

NATO allies," e.g., Israel and Pakistan; or by fudging if a nation actually has attained full nuclear status, e.g., North Korea (see Figure 2).

There are limits, however, to what this approach can accomplish. Such a weak alliance system, with its expanding set of loose affiliations, risks becoming analogous to the international system that failed to contain offensive actions prior to the First World War. Of course, unlike 1914, there is no power today that can rival the projection of U.S. conventional forces anywhere on the globe. But in a world with an increasing number of nuclear or nuclear-ready states, including Iran, North Korea, Algeria, Egypt, Japan and many others, this may not matter. In such a world, the actions of just one or two states could check U.S. influence or ignite a war Washington could have difficulty winning (see Figure 3).

Post-911

Today

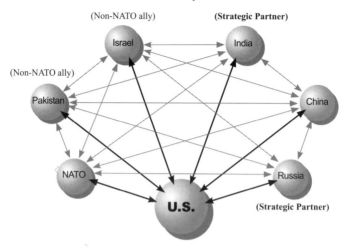

21 Possible Strategic Relationships
(6 of the most important with the U.S.)

Figure 2.

Consider Taiwan. It tried to acquire nuclear weapons several decades ago. Now, with China constantly increasing its conventional missile and amphibious strength across the Taiwan Strait, Taipei could easily have cause to try to acquire nuclear weapons again. If it were to try, China would surely demand that the United States get Taiwan to cease and desist and threaten invasion if Taiwan did not. Taipei would probably stand down—but undoubtedly would try to condition its denuclearization on having the United States produce some clear signal of security support. Would the United States blink or back Taiwan? If it expressed support for Taiwan's existence (perhaps with a forward U.S. naval deployment) and thereby defused Taiwan's nuclear proliferation moves, could the United States cope with what undoubtedly would be a sharp, threatening response from Beijing? The point of this hypothetical case is that even the slightest move by Taiwan to acquire nuclear weapons could overwhelm the strategic relationships Washington has built with China and other Asian nations over the last half-century to head off such wars.

Possible Proliferated Future
2015

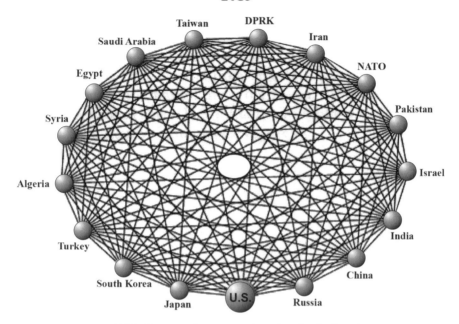

(136 chances for strategic miscalculations)

Today, plus
Iran   DPRK   Taiwan   Saudi Arabia   Egypt
Syria   Algeria   Turkey   South Korea   Japan

Figure 3.

Another case of increasing interest is that of India and Pakistan. The United States recently made Pakistan a non-NATO ally, and is in the midst of making India a strategic partner. Washington's professed aim is to bolster stability between these two nations. But how would the United States view Pakistan if another attempt on President Musharraf's life proved successful and Pakistan fell under Taliban control? At that point, a number of things would likely occur. Immediately, the political stock of the nation's current hero, Dr. Khan, would rise; indeed, there has already been talk about him succeeding Musharraf under such circumstances. If Dr. Khan did not succeed Musharraf, someone sympathetic to Dr. Khan surely would.

In any case, a Talibanized Pakistan could be counted on to work more closely with its ideological allies in the front lines in Kashmir against India and with Saudi Arabia. Riyadh—a financial backer of Pakistan's nuclear activities—is now investigating how it might acquire nuclear weapons in the likely case that Iran continues on its current nuclear course. Meanwhile, senior Pakistani military officials sympathetic to the Taliban already have suggested that Pakistan could legally base some of its nuclear warheads on Saudi soil as long as they remained under Pakistani control; a Taliban-dominated Pakistan might well implement this idea in order to achieve strategic depth for any future conventional conflict with India. If a Talibanized Pakistan ignited another war with India, China would diplomatically side with Pakistan, and the United States would side with its strategic friend, India. This would appear to create a balance. But if Pakistan thought it could count on Saudi missiles armed with Pakistani warheads to counter any Indian aggression, would Islamabad recognize this balance and be deterred?

Again, the point of this hypothetical case is that a little nuclear proliferation—in this case, from Pakistan to Saudi Arabia—could undo a considerable amount of American diplomacy and might well tip the balance toward dragging Washington into war. This set of observations suggests that nuclear terrorism, per se, may no longer be our biggest worry. Instead, the greater danger would be that with more nuclear and nuclear-ready states, the coalitions needed to check or undo nuclear terrorist efforts would be too few to be effective and the willingness of countries to toy with mortal strategic combat too great for existing efforts to keep them in check. The insufficient interest of states in fighting nuclear terrorism and their interest in strategic combat, moreover, may be mutually reinforcing. As states fail to do what is needed to stem nuclear terror, more will sense the weakness of large powers and thus be more inclined to risk nuclear brinksmanship themselves. This, in turn, would tend to reduce the willingness of nuclear-capable states to open up their own nuclear activities in order to ferret out possible terrorist schemes or proliferation networks.

Can Proliferation Be Stopped?

This is not good news, but it is hardly inevitable. Three things, in particular, could improve matters greatly. First, much more can be done to reduce the production and accessibility of weapons-usable plutonium and uranium. Terrorists seeking to explode a nuclear device need not acquire very much material: The crudest nuclear mechanism would only require 60 kilograms of highly enriched uranium, divided into two pieces, with one dropped upon the other from a height of as little as 10 feet. A plutonium bomb would require more sophistication, but Dr. Khan has made such devices easier to build by making a workable engineering design much more widely available. Even if such bombs had only a one-kiloton yield—a fraction of the explosive power of the bombs used on Japan in World War II—the effects on a densely populated city would be terrible. A recent analysis of such an attack by the Natural Resources Defense Council, in which a one-kiloton bomb was used in San Francisco, resulted in estimates that 26,000 people would be killed and another 10,000 would be injured—casualties an order of magnitude greater than the deaths on September 11. In the United States and Russia alone, there are tens of thousands of bombs-worth of highly enriched uranium and weapons-grade plutonium stored as surplus. Meanwhile, over 40,000 weapons-worth of weapons-usable civilian plutonium is being stored in Europe, India, and Japan. As President Bush has pointed out, *none* of this material or the means to make it is necessary to produce nuclear energy, and *all* of it can bring nations within days of having nuclear weapons of their own. Fortunately, safer nuclear fuels, unsuitable for weapons, are readily available; an effort to use them is urgently needed and imminently doable.

Second, we must be willing to act on first indications and early intelligence. Consider the A. Q. Khan network. We knew about some of the key actors there, not weeks ago, not years ago, but *decades* ago. We did not pursue what we knew. Many of the same names that are part of the present proliferation problem appeared in the 1981 book, *The Islamic Bomb*—the first names have sometimes changed, but the last names remain the same, as one generation has passed on the business to the next. For more than 2 decades, those who were engaged in helping Pakistan secure the bomb, and who worked with Dr. Khan to help him distribute this knowledge, were not questioned about their activities. Given the ease with which a nuclear weapon can now be made—requiring less time, money, and manpower than ever before—we no longer have the luxury of waiting to act.

Third, more should be done to raise the political and economic costs of acquiring nuclear arms or coming within weeks of doing so. The most important thing is to start reading the Nuclear Nonproliferation Treaty properly. It calls for the sharing of nuclear technology, but only in conformity with the treaty's prohibitions against doing anything to encourage or assist nonweapons states in getting nuclear weapons. President Bush is one of the very few American presidents (the others being Presidents Ford and Carter) to try to spell out what "in conformity" means. On February 11, 2004, the president laid out seven worthy proposals that would restrict or reduce the number of nations making weapons-usable plutonium or uranium.

These proposals deserve greater support both within the United States and internationally. They include taking direct action against proliferation networks using the same techniques we use to fight terrorism; strengthening the laws and international controls that govern proliferation; expanding efforts to keep dangerous materials out of the wrong hands; preventing countries like North Korea and Iran from producing weapons-grade nuclear material while pretending to work only on peaceful, civilian nuclear energy programs; and taking measures to make the IAEA stronger, more legitimate, and more decisive.

Several additional steps should be taken to sustain the president's proposals. First, we should view additional large civilian nuclear projects—including nuclear power and desalinization plants, large research reactors, and regional fuel-cycle centers—as illegitimate under the Nuclear Nonproliferation Treaty if they are not privately financed or approved after an open international bidding process against less risky alternatives. This would not only spotlight countries like Iran that refused to allow non-nuclear energy alternatives to compete openly to supply their electrical power needs; it would also discourage the United States and allied governments from building large nuclear commercialization projects and subsidizing nuclear power with billions of dollars, as was supported in the energy bill of 2005.

Second, we should get as many declared nuclear weapons states as possible formally to agree not to redeploy nuclear weapons onto any other state's soil in peacetime and not to tolerate any other nation's attempt to do so. This could help thwart rumored schemes to have Pakistan legally transfer nuclear weapons under its control to Saudi Arabia, or North Korea's threat to transfer nuclear weapons to other states. It also could help establish restraints over nuclear weapons states that have not signed the Nuclear Nonproliferation Treaty (India, Pakistan, and Israel) and allow the United States to get credit for what it has already begun to do—withdraw its unnecessary overseas basing of obsolete tactical nuclear weapons.

Finally, we should encourage the United Nations (UN) to adopt a set of country-neutral rules against any nation that the IAEA and the UN Security Council do not clearly find in full compliance with the Nuclear Nonproliferation Treaty. Rather than wait for either of these bodies to find a specific country in clear violation of the treaty and then impose particular sanctions—something these bodies are increasingly loath to do—the United States and its allies should spell out in advance the minimal steps to be taken against any country not clearly in full compliance. This recommendation would reverse the present dynamic by making it the default position of the IAEA and the Security Council to encourage complying members to take action against states that defy the rules.

A New Pillar.

These additional measures may seem ambitious. But they build on what President Bush and our allies have been doing—namely, working to establish a third major security pillar to international relations. Two pillars dominated the last 4 centuries of international politics. The first pillar is freedom of commerce, which gave rise to a common international usage against piracy. The second pillar is the humane treatment of people, which produced an international common usage against slave-trading. These pillars have justified a significant number of wars and alliances, and have powerfully shaped modern international relations.

What remains to be done, and urgently, is to create a third pillar pertaining to the further spread of strategic arms, particularly nuclear weapons. Just as piracy and slave-trading can only operate outside the protection of international law, so must the illicit trade of nuclear weapons-related goods be considered out of bounds. Ultimately, this will entail a major reorientation of international affairs. This task will not be easy. The alternative to moving in this direction, though, is far grimmer—slipping into the kind of chaos that prevailed in 1914, when a single anarchist's bullet set off a series of strategic wars that nearly snuffed out Western civilization. With nuclear weapons all around or on the ready, this is hardly a condition that anyone, even the strongest of nations, can sanely entertain.

SECTION II

NEW PROLIFERATION WORRIES

CHAPTER 4

MISSILE DEFENSE COOPERATION
AND THE MISSILE TECHNOLOGY CONTROL REGIME

Mitchell Kugler

This presentation has three key conclusions: 1) There need not be friction between the intersection of the Missile Technology Control Regime (MTCR) and international missile defense cooperation; 2) To the extent such friction exists, it is being generated by some supporters of the MTCR, though there are many people — myself included — who regard themselves both as supporters of missile defense *and* the MTCR; and, 3) To the extent a conflict between missile defense and the MTCR is generated — needlessly, in my view — it will be the MTCR that suffers.

Along with many others, I spent much time during the Clinton presidency working in support of missile defense. In 1997 I was given an opportunity to run a new subcommittee on the Senate Governmental Affairs Committee, whose principal focus was on what we thought of as the "strategic basket" of issues: missile defense, arms control, proliferation, export controls, and strategic deterrence. Under Senator Thad Cochran's chairmanship, we looked into each of these areas, shifting our attention occasionally among the various elements of the "strategic basket" while remaining faithful to the overall outlines of the basket.

Senator Cochran quite consciously defined the elements of this "strategic basket," after reflection on why missile defense was not making greater progress. Of course, the Clinton administration's absolute hostility to missile defense was a significant element of the lack of progress, but the absence of a coherent strategy by missile defense supporters allowed the administration to inhibit progress unfettered by significant opposition.

So we began in 1997 with a string of hearings on missile proliferation which, I should note, would not have been possible without the work of Dennis Ward and a Legis Fellow whose services

I was sharing with the office of Senator Jon Kyl, John Rood, whose findings were captured in *The Proliferation Primer*, a 1998 majority report of Senator Cochran's subcommittee. We focused so much on proliferation because missile defense proponents were in the habit of giving lengthy speeches on the various missile defense architectures they found attractive without explaining *why* they were convinced of the need for missile defense. By failing to make clear the fundamental need for missile defense, we were failing to attract sufficient support.

In looking back at the *Primer*, it strikes me that so little has changed in the nearly 8 years since it was published. Proliferation from Russia and China continues. What was then emerging as a serious threat, was noted as such in the *Primer*, and has now fully emerged — the phenomenon of rogue to rogue proliferation — not only continues, but shows little signs of abating.

And, of course, all of this has occurred under the regime of the MTCR. In fact, more countries have ballistic missile technology now than when the regime began. We could have an endless debate about whether in the absence of the MTCR still more would have had such technology, or whether those that possess missile technology would have had even more advanced technology than they currently possess, but that debate would miss the point: However well-intentioned and well-executed, the MTCR has not, and will not, stop the spread of missile technology. At best, it can, on occasion, slow it down; at worst, it can lull us into a false sense of security — that is, a mindset of "as it is written, so it shall be," with little regard to the facts.

Consider what the Director of Central Intelligence's (DCI) July-December 1996 report, "The Acquisition of Technology Relating to Weapons of Mass Destruction (WMD) and Advanced Conventional Munitions", said then:

- Nonproliferation . . . regimes can be deceived by determined proliferators.

- During the last half of 1996, China was the most significant supplier of WMD-related goods and technology to foreign countries. The Chinese provided a tremendous variety of assistance to both Iran's and Pakistan's ballistic missile programs.

- Russia supplied a variety of ballistic missile-related goods to foreign countries during the reporting period, especially to Iran.

Now consider some of the missile-related points in the DCI's latest report covering the period January 1-June 30, 2002:

- Chinese entities continued to provide Pakistan with missile-related technical and material assistance during the reporting period . . . . In addition, firms in China have provided dual-use missile-related items, raw materials, and/or assistance to several other countries of proliferation concern — such as Iran, Libya, and to a lesser extent, North Korea.

- Russian entities during the reporting period continued to supply a variety of ballistic missile-related goods and technical know-how to countries such as Iran, India, and China. Iran's earlier success in gaining technology and materials from Russian entities has helped to accelerate Iranian development of the *Shaab-3* medium range ballistic missile (MRBM), and continuing Russian entity assistance most likely supports Iranian efforts to develop new missiles and increase Tehran's self-sufficiency in missile production.

- Throughout the first half of 2002, North Korea continued to export significant ballistic missile-related equipment, components, materials, and technical expertise to the Middle East, South Asia, and North Africa. P'yongyang attaches high priority to the development and sale of ballistic missiles, equipment, and related technology. Exports of ballistic missiles and related technology are one of the North's major sources of hard currency, which fuel continued missile development and production.

How much has actually changed? It is important to understand just what the threat is and what it is not. Countries are not *the* threat; they are simply the threat's manifestation. *The* threat, in ballistic missile terms, is *proliferation*. So while on occasion we will eliminate a ballistic missile threat from one country or another, as has recently been done so successfully in Iraq, over time we should expect other countries to emerge as ballistic missile successors. This will happen despite the presence and best efforts of the MTCR. And it stands to reason that this will occur as hostile states seek methods by which to threaten—coerce, deter, call it what you will—the United States, its deployed forces, allies, and friends.

And thus the need for missile defense—again, despite the best efforts of the MTCR. More importantly, the need for international cooperation on missile defense, particularly in light of the Bush administration's entirely new missile defense policy to protect not only the United States and deployed forces, but also allies and friends.

In fact, international cooperation already has begun. The United States is—and has been—working with Israel on the *Arrow* interceptor for quite some time, and enhanced co-production of the interceptor is beginning in the United States. We are working with Japan on the *Standard Missile-3* (SM-3), and Japan has noted publicly its interest in working on a larger booster for the SM-3. We are working with Italy and Germany on the Medium Extended Air Defense System (MEADS) program, and with the United Kingdom on the upgrade to the early warning radar at Fylingdales. It appears that a similar upgrade, in cooperation with Denmark, will also soon begin on the Thule early warning radar. The bilateral missile defense relationship also appears to be proceeding quickly with Poland, as does the multilateral missile defense work with the North Atlantic Treaty Organization (NATO), which, in a recent major move forward, added the protection of population centers to its considerations for missile defense. So there is cooperation with six countries—Israel, England, Japan, Germany, Italy, and Denmark; expanding cooperation with NATO; and imminent cooperation with Poland, which is rapidly emerging as one of America's closest allies.

It is only with Israel, on *Arrow* cooperation, that there have been MTCR issues. I will take a moment now to comment on the most recent *Arrow* issue.

Israel is going to test the *Arrow* interceptor twice in the United States in the near future. As conducting a test in the United States is a difficult and expensive endeavor, Israel will ship four *Arrow* interceptors here to ensure the availability of two spares, should there be any problems with the test articles.

The Israelis were informed, however, that in the event their spares were not used, they would not be able to return them to Israel because the United States would, in sending them back, be transferring MTCR "category 1" items. Transferring category 1 items, while permissible under the MTCR, is considered anathema by most of the regime's supporters.

Now, consider for a moment a few relevant facts: Israel already manufactures the *Arrow* interceptor. Israel has already deployed the *Arrow* interceptor. The interceptors the United States would be sending back to Israel were already in the possession of the Israelis themselves. In sum, shipping the two spare *Arrow*s back to Israel would not in any way, shape, or form enhances the missile technology of Israel. But, unfortunately, this most recent case has demonstrated that oftentimes there exists little room for the intrusion of common sense upon the MTCR.

After examining a variety of options—to include even storing the spare *Arrow* interceptors at sea so they are not technically in the United States before shipment back to Israel—the "solution" found is for the Israelis to be in "possession" (whatever that means) of the spare *Arrow*s at all times when they are in the United States. So when these spares are shipped back to Israel, it will be Israel shipping to Israel, not the United States shipping to Israel.

This example is considered to be a "success" by many MTCR supporters. Though there are others, myself included, who find this to be the ultimate in form over substance. Indeed, I suspect this odd example should be more than sufficient for other MTCR members seeking to use U.S. actions as justification for their proliferation activities, otherwise known as "exports."

Surely supporters of the MTCR must acknowledge that this makes no sense. Would it have not been better, not to mention honest, to state simply that Israel already possesses the *Arrow* interceptor and the spares being shipped back do nothing to enhance Israel's missile capabilities? That shipping another nation's property hardly can be construed reasonably as violating the MTCR? Not to mention the fact that the United States has been supporting Israel, financially and technologically, in building *Arrow*? Or even that the United States doesn't consider missile defense to be governed by the MTCR?

Protecting the United States could, perhaps, be done only from the territory of the United States. Anything is possible. But the truth of the matter is that anything beyond a rudimentary defense requires assets placed outside of the United States. Placing assets outside of the United States, though, will not necessarily cause conflict with the MTCR. Sensors in space or radars in other countries will not conflict with the MTCR, nor will battle management or command and control assets. But what about interceptors?

I will briefly survey examples of potential international missile defense cooperation, some of which might be managed successfully under the MTCR.

1. *Interceptor cooperation falling below MTCR thresholds.* It is hard to imagine that the administration, having so recently divested itself of the Anti-ballistic Missile (ABM) Treaty—which prohibited substantive international cooperation—would now allow the MTCR to substitute for portions (i.e., Articles IX and X) of that defunct treaty. Or that the Bush administration would, in limiting interceptor cooperation to that permitted by the MTCR, essentially impose upon itself the kind of "demarcation" between permissible and impermissible cooperation that was so bitterly opposed in years past during the "theater/strategic demarcation" debates under the ABM Treaty.

2. *Basing U.S. interceptors on foreign soil but under the control of the United States.* Some of my friends with a different view than mine insist that providing missile defense for host nations in exchange for using their territory to base our interceptors should be more than sufficient for the host nation. In some instances this may be a reasonable trade. In many instances, the basing of interceptors will protect not only foreign soil, but also deployed U.S. forces, while at the same time enhancing protection for the United States itself.

3. *Receiving technological assistance from our allies and friends.* There is no denying that the United States has done a tremendous amount of research and development on missile defense, far more than any other country. But to therefore assume that no other nation could contribute its technological expertise usefully would be arrogant in the extreme. In my current position, I spend a substantial amount of time with defense companies in other countries, and I can assure you that in every one of these companies, I work with people every bit

as talented as the best in American industry. As hardware follows know-how, without question the MTCR will be an impediment here.

4. *Transferring interceptors to others.* Without question, the greatest potential for missile defense/MTCR conflict comes from this option. Some seem unwilling to accept the fact that many of our allies view themselves as sovereign nations with a responsibility for their own defense. As sovereigns, they may well object to continued U.S. control of interceptors on their soil rather than transferring the interceptors to them for their use — as we already do with so many other weapons systems.

While currently the MTCR is inhibiting *Arrow* cooperation in particular, the fact remains that *Arrow* is further along in terms of international cooperation than most of our other programs. The time for transferring other hardware will soon be upon us, along with the choices that invariably will be faced if the MTCR is left as it is now.

There are two broad options to choose from, each obviously having many permutations. We can:

1. *Declare as a matter of policy that missile defense cooperation will be excluded from the purview of the MTCR.* The United States has, after all, managed to export the D5 missile and cruise missiles despite the MTCR. Has this brought the regime to its knees? Of course it has not. But the regime has managed to continue, even though the United States is transferring an inter-continental ballistic missile (ICBM) capable of being nuclear-armed to the United Kingdom. Why, then, should transferring missile defense to the United Kingdom, or, for that matter, any other ally, pose a problem? The simple fact is that the object of the MTCR is to reduce as much as possible the flow of missile technology *to those we don't want to have such technology.* The purpose of missile defense is, among other things, for protection from the failures of the MTCR. These purposes are complementary and should not be set in opposition.

2. *Restrict cooperation to that permitted by the MTCR.* In so doing, we would occupy vast amounts of the bureaucracy's time and effort in what would be a "Groundhog Day" of missile defense fights. On each and every occasion that some form of cooperation was proposed, proponents would line up their arguments and opponents would be energized by having another opportunity to draw the line

on the primacy of the MTCR over missile defense cooperation. In some cases, cooperation would be denied; in others, as has already been the case, we would see cooperation reduced. Of course, as cited already on *Arrow*, in still other cases, some cute interpretation of the MTCR might be found such that we remain "compliant" with the regime. But I wonder of what value such a regime would be if its ideas are to be made as infinitely elastic as the government's lexicon in George Orwell's *1984*?

Colleagues of mine with opposing views frequently insist that a unilateral policy decision on the part of the United States to interpret the MTCR as permitting international missile defense cooperation will only throw open the door for any country — and these colleagues always stress "*any*" — to act however it pleases in exporting missile technology. Perhaps that is true. But I do not think so.

The menace of WMD delivered by ballistic missiles is well known today. It is more than a theory; we have seen ballistic missiles used just as we have witnessed the actions of several nations in pursuing WMD to seat atop their missiles. Countries today know — without needing the MTCR to inform them — of the danger of exporting missile technology and know-how without regard for the consequences.

Even if there were no MTCR, the United States — and like-minded nations — would be perfectly capable of doing their utmost to stem missile proliferation. So it is entirely possible that leaders of some nations will suggest that their missile proliferation is no different from that practiced by the United States, albeit ours under the "guise" of "missile defense cooperation." The United States should not accept this type of statement as having even a shred of legitimacy.

Nations may well seek to justify their missile proliferation in this manner. But in so doing, they will be offering an excuse for actions they otherwise would have taken anyway. At most, the United States will be providing a new excuse for old and illegitimate actions on the part of proliferators.

CHAPTER 5

A FRESH EXAMINATION OF THE PROLIFERATION DANGERS OF LIGHT WATER REACTORS

Victor Gilinsky

LWRs Become the Nuclear Power Workhorse around the World.

From the beginning of the nuclear age, American efforts to shape the worldwide development of nuclear energy were driven, in part, by U.S. interest in limiting the possibilities for diversion of civilian facilities to military purposes. U.S. policy went through stages, at each one of which it appeared as if a particular technological or institutional approach to nuclear energy could tame it sufficiently to allow worldwide commercial use without spreading access to nuclear weapons. But in time, the real world poked holes in one rationale after another. The subject of this chapter involves one of these technological policy initiatives, the consequences of which we are living with today—encouraging the spread, starting in the 1960s, of U.S. light water reactor (LWR) technology as the basic nuclear power workhorse throughout the world.[1]

In the 1950s, before the advent of nuclear power plants, the United States tried to control the uranium market by buying up uranium at high prices. This naturally encouraged exploration that demonstrated that uranium was plentiful and negated the U.S. effort at control. With easy access to uranium but lacking indigenous uranium enrichment facilities, Britain, France, and Canada opted for reactor designs that utilized natural uranium fuel and heavy water or graphite as the neutron moderator. In the late 1950s and early 1960s, they interested Italy, Japan, India, and other countries in heading in this direction. Not only did this threaten America's competitive position, but it also threatened to spread a type of reactor that lent itself easily to production of plutonium. In fact, the first British and French power reactors were based on their military plutonium production reactors.

America's advantage was two-fold. The United States had developed a compact, and therefore relatively low-cost, LWR design based on a naval propulsion reactor design. And the United States had invested heavily in gaseous diffusion plants in Tennessee, Kentucky, and Ohio to enrich uranium for weapons.

The LWR could only operate on enriched uranium, that is, uranium more concentrated in the active uranium-235 isotope than natural uranium.[2] By virtue of its huge enrichment capacity, the United States had an effective monopoly on the production of this fuel. Moreover, as the cost of the plants had been largely assigned to the military budget, the United States decided to sell the stuff at low prices that did not defray the massive investment. It was a price that at the time no other country could even hope to offer in the future. From the point of view of customers, it was a deal that was hard to refuse, even if it came with U.S. control conditions. Ultimately, the amount of engineering invested in these designs and the depth of experience with them overwhelmed any conceptual advantages other reactor types may have had. While not the exclusive choice—Canada and India continued developing the natural uranium/heavy water designs that evolved into the CANDU reactor—the LWR became the standard reactor type around the world. In the late 1960s, France switched to LWRs, and Britain did later. Other European manufacturers in Germany and Sweden chose LWRs. The Soviets eventually did, too. There are now over 350 LWRs in operation in the world today.[3]

From the point of view of proliferation, the advantages of the LWR were considerable as compared with natural uranium-fueled reactors. U.S. policymakers thought that the most important security advantage of LWRs was that the LWR customers knew that they risked losing their reactor fuel supply if they misused the reactors for military purposes. There appeared to be detailed technical advantages, as well. For a given size of reactor, the LWRs produced less plutonium. The plutonium was, generally speaking, more difficult to extract from the LWR fuel by chemical reprocessing because the fuel is irradiated for a longer period of time, i.e., it has a higher fuel burn-up, and hence is more radioactive, necessitating more shielding of the separation process. LWRs also had to be shut down for refueling which makes for easier oversight of the fuel, whereas most natural uranium reactors are refueled online and continually, so it is harder to keep track of the fuel elements. It was widely believed through the

1970s—even by the top people in the International Atomic Energy Agency (IAEA) in Vienna—that it was not usable at all.

It is important to correct one widely held belief about LWR spent fuel. The isotopic characteristics of spent fuel from LWRs are about the same as that of spent fuel from heavy water reactors such as the CANDU, even though the LWR burn-up is much higher. This is because of the differences in the enrichment levels of the two types of fuel. The weapons usability of plutonium from either fully irradiated LWR spent fuel or fully irradiated CANDU spent fuel would be comparable.[4]

Even the intrinsic technical advantages of the LWRs themselves do not now appear as significant as they once did. While LWRs do not produce as much plutonium as natural uranium-fueled reactors of the same size, the modern LWRs are so much bigger than the older natural uranium plants that they are also prolific plutonium producers.[5] A standard size LWR with an electrical generating capacity of about 1,000 megawatts produces about 250 kilograms of plutonium per year. (That has to be compared with the nominal five kilograms of plutonium per warhead.)

Worldwide Spread of Enrichment Technology Eases Access to Nuclear Weapons.

In any case, the proliferation benefits of worldwide deployment of LWRs gradually attenuated. Just as the market for uranium encouraged exploration that negated U.S. control, so the spread of LWRs and the consequent market for enrichment encouraged the reinvention by others of the gaseous diffusion enrichment process— originally developed by the United States during World War II—as well as the development of the gas centrifuge enrichment process. Together, these developments broke the U.S. monopoly on the supply of enrichment for LWRs.

In particular, France built a large gaseous diffusion plant, and the United Kingdom (UK), West Germany, and the Netherlands established the Urenco consortium which supplies enrichment services from gas centrifuge plants in each of these countries. While the gaseous diffusion plants in France and the United States continue to operate, both countries have announced plans to replace them with new gas centrifuge plants. Moreover, Russia long ago abandoned the gaseous diffusion process in favor of gas centrifuge and is now a major competitor for enrichment supply on the international market. Other countries which already rely or plan to rely on nuclear power to a significant extent—notably Japan and China,respectively—also have built gas centrifuge plants, although at present they do not supply enrichment services to the international market.

Global attention has been focused recently on the proliferation implications of centrifuge enrichment as a consequence of the revelations about Pakistan's role in spreading this technology. The activities of A. Q. Khan and his associates in trading the centrifuge technology he stole from Urenco to Iran, North Korea, Libya, and possibly other countries has underlined the "front-end" vulnerability of the LWR once-through fuel cycle.

An important advantage of the gas centrifuge process is that it is much less energy intensive than gaseous diffusion. The trend towards using gas centrifuge instead of gaseous diffusion for commercial enrichment also has been driven by improvements in centrifuge performance. The newer models are much more reliable and have a larger unit enrichment capacity. Gas centrifuge plants also are inherently much more flexible than gaseous diffusion plants to accommodate different combinations of feed enrichment, tails (waste) concentration, and product enrichment. Large centrifuge enrichment plants can be thought of as many smaller centrifuge plants in parallel, so the small modular units can be shifted around fairly easily, or one can stand by itself. In other words, gas centrifuge technology lends itself to small-scale operation.

Unfortunately, these characteristics also make the gas centrifuge process a much bigger proliferation risk than, say, gaseous diffusion technology. That applies both to (1) the possibility that the owner of an existing declared low enriched uranium (LEU) plant would modify it to also produce heavy enriched uranium (HEU), and (2) that someone would construct a small clandestine HEU plant.

It is now generally appreciated that gas centrifuge plants for LEU can fairly easily be turned into plants for HEU. It is less appreciated that LEU at, say, 4 percent enrichment, is about 80 percent of the way to HEU. It takes comparatively little additional "separative work" to upgrade LEU to HEU. It would be difficult for the IAEA to keep close enough track of all the LEU to stay ahead of any such conversion.

Having a gas centrifuge plants producing LEU makes it much easier to construct and operate a clandestine one. The presence of the larger plant would mask many of the intelligence indicators and environmental indications of a clandestine one so it would harder to find.

But even in the absence of any commercial enrichment—in the case of a country with one or more stand alone LWRs—the presence of LWRs means that a substantial supply of fresh LWR fuel would also be present at times. That such fresh fuel can provide a source of uranium for clandestine enrichment is another possibility that has received essentially no attention in proliferation writings. Since the fuel is already LEU, a much smaller gas centrifuge plant would suffice to raise the enrichment to bomb levels than would be the case if the starting point was natural uranium. By starting with such LEU fuel pellets, which are uranium oxide (UO_2), the enricher would be able to skip the first five processes required to go from uranium ore to uranium hexafluoride gas, the material on which the gas centrifuge operate. To go from the uranium oxide pellets to uranium hexafluoride, the would-be bombmaker would crush the pellets and react the powder with fluorine gas. Suitably processed, the LEU pellets could provide feed for clandestine enrichment.

Worldwide Spread of Reprocessing Technology for Plutonium Separation.

By contrast to the heavy attention recently directed at the possibility of clandestine uranium enrichment, there has been relatively little attention directed at the possibility of clandestine reprocessing to separate plutonium from LWR spent fuel. It is a principal concentration of this chapter.

In previous debates on the subject, the point was made that (1) plutonium contained in LWR spent fuel is unsuitable for weapons; that anyhow (2) anything short of a high-investment commercial reprocessing plant—beyond the means and capabilities of most countries — would not provide access to the plutonium contained in the LWR spent fuel; and (3) such reprocessing would be detected by international inspectors. We believe these bars to using LWRs as a source of plutonium for weapons are very much exaggerated.

Partial cores removed from an LWR after one fuel cycle (rather than the conventional three) have lower burnup and hence contain plutonium with a higher Pu-239 content than the plutonium in spent fuel of the full design burnup. Such plutonium is sometime called fuel grade, as distinguished from weapons grade at one end and reactor grade at the other. In practical effect, such plutonium is near-weapons grade. The characteristics of simple fission weapons using this material are not very different from those using weapons grade plutonium. The fuel grade plutonium is markedly superior for weapons use than reactor grade plutonium from spent fuel of the design burnup. The arguments surrounding the usability of LWR plutonium for weapons deal with the high burnup reactor grade material and so are irrelevant for the present discussion.

Reprocessing of LWR spent fuel is not particularly difficult for a country with modest technological capabilities. Witness North Korea's reprocessing of its plutonium production reactor spent fuel. While reprocessing LWR fuel is harder than reprocessing low burnup natural uranium fuel, the feasibility of small-scale, and possibly "quick and dirty" reprocessing of LWR fuel has been known for 30 years.

It is more difficult to make categorical statements regarding the ability of IAEA inspectors to detect a hypothetical clandestine reprocessing plant. Such a plant could likely remain hidden until it is put to use — until spent fuel is withdrawn from a reactor, and the reprocessing operation begins. Even if the start of operation would be detected promptly, which is by no means sure, especially as to location, it is possible that the operator of the clandestine plant could manage to produce militarily significant quantities of plutonium and weapons before the international system could react effectively. To place these issues in context, we first summarize the evolution of U.S. policy on the proliferation implications of commercial reprocessing.

1974 Indian Nuclear Explosion Sparks Policy Debate over LWRs and Reprocessing.

The reasons for addressing these matters now—the reason for a fresh look—are that firmly held but erroneous views on the facts underlie important U.S. policies on LWRs. Until 2001, the State Department defended putting LWRs in North Korea as part of the 1994 U.S.-Democratic People's Republic of Korea (DPRK) Agreed Framework on the grounds that LWRs were "proliferation resistant"—that North Korea would find it difficult, if not impossible, to reprocess LWR spent fuel. Even now, that U.S.-supported project is only suspended, not terminated.

The State Department's Russian counterparts made similar arguments, and continue to make them, in supporting the Russian construction of Bushehr reactors in Iran. And even in arguing against the Russian power reactor project at Bushehr on proliferation grounds, the United States says only that the civilian project could provide cover for a clandestine Iranian bomb effort, not that the plant itself is inherently dangerous.

The LWR issues also have much wider significance. The idea that plutonium from LWRs is unusable for bombs is an essential underpinning of the commercial drive for worldwide deployment of LWRs.

It has long been understood that the most difficult hurdle for a country seeking nuclear weapons is getting the nuclear explosive materials—either HEU or plutonium. By comparison, the design and fabrication of the nuclear weapon itself poses a less difficult obstacle. That is why the technologies that extract the nuclear explosive material—uranium enrichment and reprocessing—are designated as "sensitive" technologies in the polite international discussions over nuclear controls against proliferation. In plain language, "sensitive" means dangerous.

The 1974 Indian nuclear explosion alerted the United States to the ease with which a country that had reactors and reprocessing could progress to nuclear weapons.[6] It also alerted those concerned with the spread of nuclear weapons of the extent to which reprocessing technology had spread and was spreading further. Even though it was equally dangerous, the United States had never restricted its reprocessing technology the way it had restricted enrichment technology. Perhaps this was because the United States could hope to maintain a commercial monopoly on uranium enrichment whereas that was unrealistic in the case of reprocessing. It was assumed in the early days of nuclear power that uranium was scarce and that reprocessing was an essential part of all reactor operation. In the background was the near-universal notion that the future of nuclear power lay in plutonium-fueled reactors, that uranium-burning reactors were just a transition phase, so cutting off access to plutonium was thought tantamount to putting a lid on the expansion of nuclear energy.[7]

The United States revealed extensive information on reprocessing at the 1955 Geneva Atoms for Peace Conference. Under the Atoms for Peace program, the United States trained many foreigners in reprocessing technology at U.S. national laboratories, such as the Oak Ridge National Laboratory and the Argonne National Laboratory that did pioneering work in reprocessing. That is where the Indian and Pakistani reprocessing experts got their start.[8] The U.S. Atomic Energy Commission, and later the Department of Energy, published encyclopedic technical volumes on the subject as well as detailed engineering reports that explicated reprocessing "know how."[9]

None of this was in any way prohibited by the Nuclear Nonproliferation Treaty (NPT) *as it was then universally interpreted*, even though it was at odds with the purpose of the treaty. According to the prevailing interpretation of the treaty, nuclear technology that was labeled by its owner as "peaceful," had some possible civilian application, and was subject to inspection by the IAEA, was deemed to be legitimate. This was so even if the technology—say, reprocessing or enrichment—brought the owner to the threshold of nuclear weapons. At that time, the real role of the IAEA inspectors was to legitimize trade rather than to find wrong-doing. The view was that international nuclear gentlemen did not inquire too deeply into the affairs of other nuclear gentlemen, and in any case, kept what they learned to themselves.[10]

In its public pronouncements the U.S. Government more or less stuck to the position that the NPT legitimized all "peaceful" nuclear activities. At the same time, the government could not ignore the dire security implications—post-1974 Indian nuclear explosion—of unrestricted commerce in nuclear technology, even if it was subject to IAEA inspection. France was then negotiating with Pakistan for the export of a reprocessing plant, and Germany was pursuing a package deal with Brazil that involved both reprocessing and enrichment technology.[11] A complication at the time was that France was not yet an NPT member. To help introduce a common set of export guidelines that included "restraint" in the export of "sensitive" technology, the United States organized the Nuclear Suppliers Group of nuclear exporting countries, initially 15 of them. This group operated, and continues to operate, as a kind of extra-treaty backstop for the NPT. The main concern at the time of its founding was that technology providing access to plutonium as uranium enrichment technology was still tightly held.[12] There were some important U.S. successes, among them stopping the French sale of a reprocessing plant to Pakistan, which France finally abandoned in 1978.[13]

What the United States should do about reprocessing and plutonium use, both domestically and internationally, became an election year issue in 1976. President Gerald Ford issued a nuclear policy statement that plutonium was at the root of the security problem associated with nuclear energy. Once separated from the radioactive waste contained in spent fuel, the material could rapidly be put to military use. President Ford stated that reprocessing—that is, chemical separation of plutonium—"should not proceed unless there is a sound reason to conclude that the world community can effectively overcome the associated risks of proliferation." In perhaps his boldest step, he announced that the United States would act domestically in a way that was consistent with what we asked of others. The United States, in its energy planning, would no longer assume future reliance on plutonium fuel. He said that he believed that we could make use of nuclear energy, and even increase reliance on it, with this security restriction. "We must be sure," he said, "that all nations recognize that the U.S. believes that nonproliferation objectives must take precedence over economic and energy benefits, if a choice must be made." To this day, U.S. policy on spent fuel assumes that it will be disposed of in a repository on a "once through" basis—that is, without reprocessing—although the current reason for this probably has more to do with economics than with security.

Gerald Ford lost the 1976 election to Jimmy Carter, and, as a consequence, it is Carter's name that usually attaches to the origin of a restrictive U.S. nonproliferation policy with respect to plutonium. Unfortunately, President Carter's erratic style and his administration's tendency to equate saying something with doing it left U.S. nonproliferation policy in a confused state that did not engender respect either at home or abroad.[14] At first, Carter took a rigid antiproliferation stance on a number of key issues, but abandoned these positions one after another when they met with domestic and international criticism, most particularly with respect to reprocessing and future use of plutonium.[15] Subsequent presidents watered down further U.S. policy on disapproval of foreign reprocessing so that it is now barely perceptible except as regards countries of direct and near-term proliferation concern and which the United States considers hostile.

What has remained, however, is the view—agreed to over the entire spectrum of nuclear opinion—that if commercial reprocessing is not present in a country, then the reactors themselves do not pose a proliferation danger. Gerald Ford drew a sensible distinction between what is too dangerous for the arteries of commerce (that is, separated plutonium) and what in the circumstances was a reasonably acceptable alternative (a once-through uranium fuel cycle). Over time, the reasonably acceptable came to be described as entirely satisfactory. This view, however, ignores some stubborn technical facts that have been know for decades, but unfortunately forgotten, about the ease and rapidity with which a country could reprocess LWR spent fuel and about the usability of such plutonium for bombs. That is the reason for a fresh look at this subject.

1976-1977 Ford-Carter Restrictive Policy on Commercial Reprocessing Leads to Debate over Clandestine Reprocessing.

Generally speaking, the nuclear industry and the nuclear bureaucracies in the Department of Energy and elsewhere did not support the once-through nuclear fuel cycle that avoided reprocessing. Ironically, industry saved a lot of money over the last nearly 30 years by adopting this approach, however reluctantly, because commercial reprocessing and recycle of plutonium as fuel is highly uneconomical.[16] Mostly, the defense of commercial reprocessing was based on the arguments that Ford and Carter had exaggerated the dangers—that so long as the commercial activities were subject to IAEA inspection (which went by, and continues to go by, the misleading name of "safeguards"), there was nothing to worry about. And, it was said in further defense of reprocessing, that the plutonium from LWRs was unsuitable for bombs and was therefore not a source of worry.[17] Both of these points are wrong, and we will devote special attention in this report to the latter one.

For the present, however, we are more interested in a different line of argument against the Ford-Carter policy supporting a once-through fuel cycle. These critics argued that banning commercial reprocessing would not provide any additional security because, anyhow, it was easy to extract the plutonium from spent fuel using small jerry-built plants that most countries could build quickly and secretly. Although they did not put it that way, they argued, in effect, that, if a country had nuclear power reactors, things were much *worse* than the new Carter administration thought.[18] This line of argument was based on an informal technical report written in 1977 by reprocessing experts at the Oak Ridge National Laboratory that presented a design for a small, quickly-built simple reprocessing plant that the designers thought could be hidden easily.[19] The argument based on this report did not gain much traction because the nuclear industry was reluctant to support an argument that, if taken seriously, could lead to the conclusion that nuclear reactors were, themselves, too dangerous to operate on a commercial basis. And supporters of the once-through approach tended to write off the significance of the Oak Ridge report in the context of the arguments over allowing large-scale commercial reprocessing. The report may have overstated to an extent the ease with which LWR spent fuel could be reprocessed quickly and secretly, but it and a number of other subsequent studies on small-scale and clandestine reprocessing made an important point. It is that LWRs operating on a commercial once-through fuel cycle—with no commercial reprocessing—are not as safe a proposition from the point of view of proliferation as they were made out to be.

A Number of Studies on "Quick and Dirty" Clandestine Reprocessing for Bombs Suggest This Is a Feasible Option.

There have been a number of studies on small-scale reprocessing, but perhaps none that received comparable attention and none that involved persons as prominent in the field as the 1977 Oak Ridge study. The godfather of the study was Floyd Culler, then Oak Ridge assistant director and a leading developer of PUREX technology. He assembled a team to prove that a country with a minimal industrial base could quickly and secretly build a small reprocessing plant capable of extracting about a bomb's worth of plutonium per day.

The response came in the previously-cited 1977 Oak Ridge memorandum that presented a design for such a plant, together with a flow sheet and equipment list with dimensions and specifications. The main technical references were from standard textbooks and handbooks.

The equipment is chosen with a several-month campaign in mind rather than long-term operation so, for example, plastic pipe can serve in places where steel pipe would be used in a commercial plant. A plant diagram attached to the memorandum and keyed to the equipment list shows the plant equipment layout from the receiving pool for radioactive spent fuel to the metal reduction furnaces for producing plutonium metal "buttons."[20] The structure housing the entire operation would be about 130 feet long and much less wide. Although they describe the plant as a "quick and dirty" one, the designers went to some pains to contain the radioactive wastes and to filter the effluents both for reasons of safety and to avoid detection.

The study concluded the plant could be in operation 4 to 6 months from the start of construction, with the first 10 kilograms of plutonium metal (about two bombs' worth) produced about 1 week after the start of operation. Once in operation, the small plant could process about one PWR assembly per day, which translates into production of about five kilograms of plutonium per day.

If one accepts this conclusion about the possible performance of such a "quick and dirty plant" or something close to it, the implications are very far-reaching concerning the risks posed by LWRs in countries interested in obtaining nuclear weapons. There would be little chance of detecting such a plant until it was in operation and spent fuel to be processed was missing from a power reactor storage pool. Given the short process time—a few days from delivery of spent fuel to plutonium metal—IAEA inspectors would have little chance of detecting a diversion and start of reprocessing under the current approach. From metal plutonium to weapon components is a matter of days. The IAEA guidelines for LWR inspections assume that from LWR spent fuel to metal weapons components takes about 1-3 months,[21] but the Agency's resource limitations and the resistance of member countries keep the actual inspection frequency of LWR inspections lower than once every 3 months. Therefore, if the Oak Ridge design or something similar would work as planned—start up quickly and then produce about a bomb's worth of plutonium a day—the operator could produce dozens of bombs before the IAEA could count on detecting it, at least using the current inspection approach.

This conclusion assumes, of course, that the reactor operator cooperates with the would-be bombmakers. It also assumes that weapon design and readiness for fabrication would be prepared in advance. Both of the latter are difficult to detect and, when detected, are often clouded in ambiguity. In any case, such detection in the past has not led to drastic international action to halt nuclear activity in the country. The history of nuclear activities in Iraq, North Korea, and Iran suggests that the time-scale for international enforcement actions is more typically on the order of years. The George W. Bush administration's tougher approach on "weapons of mass destruction" and the preventive invasion of Iraq point in a different direction. But what the lesson from that experience will be, and what policy will emerge toward countries suspected of nuclear weapon ambitions, is yet unclear. The difficulties of coping with post-invasion Iraq suggest that the United States is likely to be slower on the trigger in the future.

In view of the potentially far-reaching implications of the Oak Ridge report, the General Accounting Office (GAO) prepared an evaluation for Congress.[22] The GAO examined reviews of the Oak Ridge memorandum by five Federal agencies and a number of individuals.[23] It raised questions about how quickly the plant could be built and to what extent it could be hidden, but concluded it was a credible possibility for an experienced group of reprocessing engineers and operators. In other words, one cannot assume that a country interested in nuclear weapons will be barred from extracting militarily significant amounts of plutonium from its LWRs simply because it lacks a commercial reprocessing capability.

On the question of detectability, since 1977 we have greatly improved intelligence—for example, in the case of overhead photography and chemical analysis of environmental samples. Yet intelligence on Iraq's nuclear program was caught flat-footed in 1991 (and, of course, the IAEA completely missed the weapons program) and then was wildly off the mark in 2003. North Korea's uranium enrichment facilities have not been found. And Iran's enrichment plant was located only after a dissident Iranian group specified the coordinates.[24] There are probably more people around today skilled in the arts of reprocessing, and they have more information to work with. Additionally, we have learned that NPT membership does not guarantee performance—Iraq and North Korea violated the Treaty, and very likely Iran did as well.

Since the publication of the Oak Ridge report, other studies have been published that also consider the issue of the credibility of clandestine small-scale LWR reprocessing. The subject of clandestine plutonium extraction was addressed in a 1995 Livermore report which states that "plutonium can be separated from spent nuclear fuel with modest facilities and equipment."[25] This tracks fairly closely with the conclusions of the Oak Ridge study.

In 1996, a Sandia National Laboratories team produced a design for a small plant for reprocessing LWR spent fuel quickly and secretly.[26] They characterized it as ". . . a relatively simple process that might be operated by an adversarial group in makeshift or temporary facilities such as a remotely located warehouse or a small industrial plant." The estimated preparation lead-time for producing the first kilograms of plutonium employing a staff of six technicians was about 8 months, which is even more optimistic than that of the Oak Ridge team about 20 years earlier.

The Oak Ridge and Sandia proposals are both bare bones paper designs about which some reservation is appropriate. Both processes differ in some important respects from the standard PUREX process flow sheet. Also, no information is provided on crucial matters such as control instrumentation. This is not a process that inexperienced, even if competent, persons could handle easily. Spent fuel reprocessing is among the most sophisticated chemical engineering processes and making it work takes a good deal of know-how. But even the critics of the practicality of the Oak Ridge design all thought that the highly skilled and experienced Oak Ridge team could have made it work.

In this context, it is also worth mentioning a much earlier commercial design that does not cut corners. In the late 1950s, the Phillips Petroleum Company made a very detailed feasibility study of a small PUREX plant designed to reprocess per day about one-third ton of LWR spent fuel. It was designed to handle spent fuel whose burnup is roughly that of current LWR fuel after one refueling cycle (as opposed to the normal three).[27] The plant's head end used an underwater saw to free the fuel pins from the fuel assembly and a mechanical shear to chop individual fuel pins into small pieces. One of the striking features of the plant is its small size, about 65 feet square.[28]

It is credible for states with an industrial base and nuclear infrastructure needed to operate LWRs to construct and operate such reprocessing plants "without cutting corners" to produce significant quantities of plutonium as quickly as possible without detection.[29] Whether or not a country might opt for a "quick and dirty design facility," it would have the possibility of building one with a lower probability of malfunction and with smaller tell-tale releases.

Before we consider the policy implications of the possibility of quick and dirty reprocessing for the use of LWRs, let us pursue the question of the suitability of LWR plutonium for weapons.

Contrary to Conventional Wisdom, LWRs Can Be a Copious Source of Near-Weapons Grade Plutonium Suitable for Bombs.

Since the beginning of the nuclear age, it has been difficult to rationalize the widespread use of uranium-fueled reactors that — inescapably — produce plutonium, which is one of the two key nuclear explosives. The 1946 Acheson-Lilienthal plan, that required "dangerous" nuclear activities to be used only under international auspices, did contemplate that uranium-fueled reactors would be in national hands. The authors' rationale was that the plutonium produced by these reactors could be "denatured" to make it unusable for military application. They did not spell out the scientific basis for the denaturing they had in mind, but it appears to have been the idea that the isotopic composition of plutonium formed in reactor fuel that had been irradiated for an extended time would be unusable for bombs. The notion is wrong, but it is understandable that it would have appeared plausible at that early point.

During the World War II Manhattan Project, it was discovered that just as a uranium-238 nucleus can absorb a neutron to form plutonium-239, so the plutonium-239 can absorb a neutron to form plutonium-240.[30] The longer the uranium fuel is irradiated in a reactor to form plutonium-239, the more of the plutonium-239 will convert into plutonium-240. This isotope fissions spontaneously and releases neutrons which tend to "pre-initiate" nuclear explosions as soon as the mass of nuclear explosive is in a "critical" configuration. It is this effect that made it impossible to use plutonium in a gun-type nuclear device (as it is possible to do with uranium-235 and was, in fact, the design used in the Hiroshima bomb). It was not possible to use a gun to bring two pieces of plutonium together fast enough. As soon as they got close enough to form a critical mass, the spontaneous neutrons from plutonium-240 would set off a chain reaction whose heat would blow the pieces apart before the nuclear yield was significant.

It was this stumbling block that led to a focus on the implosion design—using high explosives to drive the nuclear explosive rapidly inward to form a dense super-critical mass. The speed of the process reduces the chance of pre-initiation. Even so, an unwanted pre-initiation that appears early in the compression can set off a premature chain reaction and limit the yield to a "fizzle yield." To reduce the chance of this, the plutonium used in the first U.S. warheads was produced in uranium fuel that had been lightly irradiated to keep the fraction of plutonium-240 at about 1 percent. In an implosion design, however, the fizzle yield, while not optimal, is still large—in the case of the first Trinity explosion it was about 1 kiloton, which it is useful to recall is one thousand *tons* of high explosives. In short, the trouble with the idea that higher plutonium-240 content would only produce a fizzle is that the fizzle yield is still pretty large.

Since the time of the Acheson-Lilienthal report, weapons designers have learned to work around the pre-initiation problem to achieve high yields with the lower quality plutonium. In time, as advanced weapon designs made the pre-initiation problem more or less irrelevant, the U.S. weapons complex settled on plutonium with a plutonium-240 content of about 7 percent (and thus a plutonium-239 content of about 93 percent) as a reasonable compromise between quality and production rate. Plutonium of this isotopic content, or something close to it, say in the range of 90 percent, is termed weapons-grade.

That the denaturing argument was not valid in technical terms did not dissuade those who found it convenient for rationalizing commercial plutonium activities from using it. The idea permeated the technological permissiveness of the 1950s Atoms for Peace program when it came to plutonium extraction and application. One could say that the false security of denaturing plutonium underlay the whole Atoms for Peace program.[31]

After the Indian nuclear explosion in 1974 that used high isotopic purity plutonium extracted from the spent fuel of a Canadian-supplied research reactor, the United States woke up to fact that misinformation in the international nuclear community downplaying the dangers of commercial plutonium was standing in the way of effective security measures. By this time, commercial LWR fuels were fairly highly irradiated during commercial operation, and the notion gained currency that the plutonium in such fuel, "reactor-grade" plutonium, was not usable at all for bombs. The Ford administration felt compelled to brief foreign nuclear leaders to correct this view and arranged for Dr. Robert Selden of the Livermore laboratory to present the material.[32] Selden's summary slide stated: "Reactor grade plutonium is an entirely credible fissile material for nuclear explosives."[33]

But despite numerous reports and analyses that addressed the issue and arrived at the same result, the controversy would not die because so much was at stake commercially and bureaucratically in the hundreds of LWRs deployed throughout the world and, in some countries, in the reprocessing and recycle of LWR plutonium.[34]

Rather than pursue this argument which seems to have reached a stalemate, the approach we take here is to circumvent it by pointing out that LWRs can also be copious producers of near-weapons-grade plutonium and even of weapons-grade plutonium itself. To explain the difference between our point of view and the conventional one regarding LWR plutonium, we have to say a few words about the way an LWR is fueled.

A PWR core, to use a specific example, may contain about 75 tons of uranium.[35] The operators refuel the reactor about every 18 months. The fuel elements normally stay in the reactor for three fuel cycles, or about 60 months. But the refueling schedule is staggered so that at each refueling, the operators take out one-third of the fuel assemblies — the ones that have been in the core for three cycles — and replace them with fresh fuel.

The conventional characterization of the isotopic composition of the plutonium contained in LWR spent fuel — so-called reactor grade plutonium — is of fuel that has been in the reactor for a full three fuel cycles. This is the LWR plutonium over which arguments have raged concerning its usability for weapons. Such fuel indeed has a high content of isotopes other than the most desirable plutonium-239. There is a certain logic in this characterization in that most of the LWR spent fuel in storage pools at LWRs contains this type of plutonium, and the LWR-bred plutonium that has been separated in reprocessing plants is more-or-less of this composition, too.[36]

But an LWR operator seeking better plutonium for weapons is not constrained to using the plutonium from irradiated fuel assemblies. For example, if the operator of a newly operating LWR unloaded the entire core after 8 months or so, the contained plutonium would be weapons-grade — with a plutonium-239 content of about 90 percent. The amount of plutonium produced would be about 2 kilograms per ton of uranium, or about 150 kilograms per 8-month cycle.[37] This comes to about 30 bombs' worth. Does a would-be nuclear weapons state need more? If the short refueling cycles were continued, the annual output of weapons-grade plutonium would be about 200 kilograms (allowing for refueling time), but this would require a large amount of fresh fuel. Such an progression involves a considerable departure from commercial operation and, for an NPT member, would signal treaty violation. Still, it illustrates what a standard LWR can do when viewed as a plutonium production reactor.

The small Oak Ridge-designed reprocessing plant described earlier would have difficulty keeping up with this kind of reactor operation for long because it was not designed for reliable long-term operation. But suppose we just consider one run of 8 months. The small reprocessing plant was designed to handle about one assembly per day. To reprocess the entire core of 177 fuel assemblies in our example would take about 6 months of operating time plus some realistic amount of down time. In less than a year, the would-be nuclear weapons country would have about 30 bombs' worth. That is quite an arsenal.

Consider a mode of operation closer to commercial operation. Because of the staggering of the refueling, at any refueling once the reactor has been operating for a time, one-third of the core (about 25 tons in our example) will have been in the reactor for three cycles, one-third will have been in the reactor for two cycles, and one-third will have been in the reactor for one cycle. The plutonium in the one-cycle fuel would have a much higher content of the most desirable plutonium-239 isotope than the three-cycle fuel—over 80 percent as opposed to about 55 percent. This plutonium is often called "fuel-grade" to distinguish it from the better weapons-grade stuff and the less desirable reactor-grade.[38] At each normal refueling, the operator has available 25 tons of uranium containing about 5 kilograms plutonium per ton, or about 125 kilograms of plutonium with about 80 percent plutonium-239—not bad material for bombs. (There is more plutonium per ton than in the earlier example because the irradiation time is longer.) In fact, this characterization understates the usefulness of the one-cycle material for weapons because what really counts is the amount fissile fraction—the sum of plutonium-239 and plutonium-241—which, in the case of spent fuel removed after one refueling cycle, is nearly 85 percent.

Even more interesting is an example we will consider in detail— the situation at the start of operation. We shall examine the weapons characteristics of the plutonium produced in the first core after the start of operation and will compare that with the characteristics of weapons-grade plutonium. At the end of the first refueling cycle, *all* the fuel will have been irradiated for only one cycle. The first cycle is also normally a bit shorter than the later ones, so the plutonium is even higher in plutonium-239 content — about 84 percent plutonium-239. At the end of the first cycle, the 75-ton core will contain about 330 kilograms of plutonium, or more than 60 weapons' worth. According to its designers, it would take the Oak Ridge plant about 150 days of operation to reprocess the entire core.

One might say that this kind of operation in violation of the NPT would not be allowed, that the international community, or perhaps some country, would step in to prevent it. Yet North Korea is believed to have reprocessed the missing 8,000 fuel rods from its small reactor, and there has been no world response. Suppose they had by now had in operation the LWRs that the United States promised them under the 1994 U.S.-DPRK Agreed Framework and had operated them in the way outlined above. Can we be confident that there would be international action to enforce the NPT rules?

How good would the first core plutonium be for weapons? The usual standard of comparison is U.S. weapons-grade plutonium, which is nominally taken to contain about 93 percent plutonium-239. How different, then, are the weapons characteristics of the plutonium in the fuel after the first cycle as compared with weapons-grade plutonium? The Nonproliferation Policy Education Center (NPEC) asked Dr. Harmon W. Hubbard, an experienced physicist who had worked on nuclear weapons at the Livermore Laboratory and served for several years on the panel that evaluated foreign nuclear explosions for the U.S. Government, to examine the issue relying on publicly available information.

The subject of illegal construction of nuclear explosives also was earlier reviewed in technical detail by J. Carson Mark, late T-Division head at Los Alamos National Laboratory (LANL), in a 1990 report.[39] He concluded that the difficulties encountered in using reactor-grade plutonium for explosive fabrication differ only in degree, but not in kind, from the problems in using weapons grade plutonium.

In his 2003 paper, Hubbard develops the calculations for the better grade of plutonium available in spent fuel after irradiation for the first fuel cycle to see how this plutonium compares in weapons use with weapons-grade plutonium. Hubbard assumes the simplest design for a first effort explosive, one consisting of a solid plutonium spherical core. This core is very nearly a critical mass when surrounded by a high density tamping (that is, neutron reflecting) material which is taken here to be uranium. This larger sphere is then encased in the high explosive system which is designed to provide a converging spherical shock wave that would compress the assembly for a few microseconds before it flies apart from the force of the nuclear explosion.

Then, based on the published Trinity data, Hubbard calculates probabilities of yields to be expected from reactor grade plutonium. He then extends these probabilistic yield estimates to improved implosion technology by adjusting a parameter in the model. One might think of these steps as increases in the speed with which the core is compressed, although some other aspects of design are involved as well. He carries out the yield calculations for first-cycle LWR plutonium and for weapons-grade plutonium.

Although the weapons-grade plutonium has less of it, both materials have some plutonium-240 that spontaneously emits neutrons. These spontaneous neutrons can start the chain reaction prematurely and cause the nuclear explosion to blow the bomb apart before the plutonium core reaches maximum compression. Hubbard takes weapons-grade material that contains 6 percent plutonium-240 (and thus 93.5 percent plutonium-239 and 0.5 percent plutonium-241, which is more-or-less equivalent for explosive purposes) and first cycle LWR plutonium that contains 14 percent plutonium-240 (and 84 percent plutonium-239 and 2 percent plutonium-241). In both cases, there is some spread in resultant yields — more in the case of first cycle LWR plutonium because it contains more plutonium-240, but not dramatically so.

The following table sums up the results of the calculations. The entries in the first three columns give the probabilities that the design will achieve an explosive yield in the ranges: 1 to 5 kilotons, 5 to 20 kilotons, and greater than 20 kilotons (the nominal yield of the 1945 Trinity shot in the New Mexico desert). The first row gives the probabilities for the Trinity design using the type of plutonium that was actually used at the time. This might be termed "super-grade" as the plutonium-240 content was only about 1 percent. The following three rows provide the same estimates for three levels of bomb technology: the 1945 Trinity technology, a two-fold (100 percent) improvement in that technology, and a three-fold improvement (200 percent). In each case, the results are presented for weapons-grade plutonium and for first-cycle LWR plutonium (bold). So, for example, the probability that a bomb using 1945 Trinity technology and first-cycle LWR plutonium would exceed 20 kilotons in yield is 12 percent. If we drop to the next row — that provides the probabilities for a two-fold improvement in the 1945 technology — we find that the probability of exceeding 20 kilotons becomes 34 percent, or about one-third. And if we drop to the last row — that assumes a three-fold technology improvement — the probability of exceeding 20 kilotons with first cycle LWR plutonium is 49 percent, or almost one-half.

	% Probability that Yield is Between 1 and 5 Kilotons: Percent	% Probability that Yield is Between 5 and 20 Kilotons: Percent	% Probability that Yield is Not Less Than 20 Kilotons: Percent	Estimated Average Yield in Kilotons: Percent
1945 Trinity shot 1% plutonium-240 (actual) Calculated:	4	6	88	19
Trinity technology WGPu	21	23	44	13
1st cycle LWR	**36**	**23**	**12**	**5**
Trinity technology x 2 WGPu	12	14	66	15
1st cycle LWR	**25**	**25**	**34**	**10**
Trinity technology x 3 WGPu	8	12	76	16
1st cycle LWR	**18**	**22**	**49**	**12**

Table 1. Probability of Achieving Various Explosive Yields and the Expected Yield for 1945 U.S. Technology and for Two Improved Levels Using Weapons Grade Plutonium (WGPu) and 1ˢᵗ Cycle LWR Plutonium.

The last column is especially interesting. It provides rough estimates of the average yield of the specific weapon design and plutonium quality combinations listed on the left. Even though there is some uncertainty in yield, the average yields are quite substantial, and the differences between weapons-grade and first-cycle LWR plutonium becomes very much less as technology is improved (that is, moving down in Table 1).

A country attempting to build nuclear weapons today could take advantage of the wide availability of declassified nuclear weapons information and the enormous increases in computing and other technological aids since the 1945 Trinity shot. It seems reasonable to attribute to a new group at least a doubling of the efficacy of the Trinity implosion system through the use of advances in implosion technology, initiators, and better core design.[40] At this level of design, a would-be nuclear state could use first-cycle LWR plutonium to produce fission weapons with a modestly reliable yield around an average of about 10 kilotons. A weapon of this design would have about a 70 percent chance of exceeding five kilotons. It should be remembered that the minimum, or fizzle, yields will likely be at least as large as that of Trinity—around one kiloton—and that this guaranteed yield already is quite destructive. Considering that the destructive radius of the explosions varies roughly as the third root of the yield, the differences between the performance of weapons with first-cycle plutonium and those with weapons-grade plutonium are not very great.

LWRS Are Less Proliferation-Resistant than Usually Assumed in Policy Discussions and Are Dangerous in the Wrong Hands.

What emerges from this discussion is that LWRs are not the proliferation-resistant technology they have been made out to be. Forgotten from the earlier days of nuclear energy is that LWRs can produce large quantities of near-weapons-grade plutonium, and that a country bent on making bombs would not have much trouble extracting it quickly in a small reprocessing operation, and possibly even keeping the operation secret until it had an arsenal.

The possibility of clandestine centrifuge enrichment exists even in the absence of a nuclear power program. Pakistan pursued enrichment before it had any reactors that used enriched uranium fuel. But a nuclear power program provides resources and makes it easier to mask a clandestine enrichment program. There is, however, one respect in which the presence of an LWR offers added opportunities for clandestine enrichment. Fresh LWR fuel, which typically has an enrichment level (uranium-235 concentration) of 4 percent, can, after crushing and fluorination, itself be used as feed for a clandestine gas centrifuge enrichment operation. Use of such low enriched feed, as opposed to natural uranium with a uranium-235 concentration of less than 1 percent, can reduce the enrichment effort by a factor of five.

In other words, LWRs themselves pose a large security issue if they are in the wrong hands. It would be useful for informing U.S. policy to gain a clearer understanding of the extent to which near-weapons grade plutonium is readily available from these reactors. Two specific examples stand out of nuclear policy inadequately informed by an understanding of the technical possibilities.

The first is the confused and inconsistent policy toward North Korea which included promising, as part of a 1994 U.S.-DPRK nuclear deal, two large LWRs whose plutonium production capacity turned out to be larger than that of all the indigenous North Korean reactors they were supposed to replace. When this came to light, the State Department insisted that the North Koreans would not have the technology to extract the LWR plutonium.

The second example involves Iran. The United States opposes Russian supply of LWRs at Bushehr, but does so on the grounds that the nuclear project can serve as a cover for clandestine nuclear activities. There does not seem to be recognition yet that the LWRs could themselves be a copious source of plutonium for weapons, or their possible link with enrichment.

Altogether, underestimating the production capacity of LWRs for weapons-grade and near weapons-grade plutonium and overestimating the difficulty of "quick and dirty" reprocessing have contributed to poor decisions.

Several broad policy implications of the weapons-grade production capability of LWRs are:

1. *Role of LWRs*. The need to reassess the role of LWRs in international programs. They are not for everyone, and we should be cautious about promoting their construction in worrisome countries. This is not a benign technology. At a minimum, we should not support such technology where it is not clearly economic.

2. *Clandestine enrichment and reprocessing*. The IAEA and national intelligence constantly has to be on the lookout for clandestine plants

because they can rapidly change the security equation. There needs to be much closer accounting of LEU fuel in view of its significance as possible feed for clandestine enrichment.

3. *IAEA inspection of LWRs.* Increase IAEA inspection frequencies for LWRs to check on fuel inventories and whether refueling needs adjustment upward in countries of concern from the point of view of potential bombmaking and to take account of possible undiscovered clandestine reprocessing. Because of inevitable IAEA resource limitations, it is necessary for the agency to concentrate inspections where they are most important. It would help to gain support for such a system if it were possible to develop some objective way of defining "countries of concern." The IAEA should take greater account of the presence of weapons-grade plutonium or near weapons-grade plutonium in spent fuel pools and storage in devising its inspections.

4. *Enforcement.* The NPT members must enforce the IAEA inspection system. An important purpose of IAEA safeguards is to deter nuclear weapons activities—by would-be nuclear weapon countries—by the threat of early detection. This assumes there will be a strong reaction to such an early detection of illicit activity. If would-be bombmakers conclude they have nothing to fear because the international community is not likely to react to their violations, the whole system of control falls apart.

ENDNOTES - CHAPTER 5

1. As nearly every interested person knows by now, light water in this context is just plain water, so called in the early days of the nuclear era to distinguish it from heavy water, in which the hydrogen atom is replaced by deuterium. LWRs come in two basic types—Pressurized Water Reactors (PWRs) and Boiling Water Reactors (BWRs). In a PWR, the nuclear core heats a pressurized primary water loop that passes through a steam generator that boils a secondary water loop to provide steam to the electric turbines. In a BWR, the water boils in the nuclear vessel and passes directly to the steam turbine. Most of the LWRs in the world are PWRs. For our purposes, the differences between PWRs and BWRs are not significant.

2. Natural uranium contains about 0.7 percent uranium-235 and 99.3 percent uranium-238. LWR fuel is normally enriched to about 4 percent, while bomb material is usually enriched to about 90 percent uranium-235.

3. There are LWRs in Armenia, Belgium, Brazil, Bulgaria, China, Czech Republic, Finland, France, Germany, Hungary, India, Japan, South Korea, Mexico, Netherlands, Russia, Slovakia, Slovenia, South Africa, Spain, Sweden, Switzerland, Taiwan, UK, and the United States.

4. The relevant figures for the percentage composition of plutonium in spent LWR and HWR fuels are given in the chart below:

Isotope	CANDU 7,500 MWD/MT	BWR 27,500 MWD/MT	PWR 33,000 MWD/MT
Pu-238	0.1	1.0	1.5
Pu-239	68.4	57.2	55.7
Pu-240	25.6	25.7	24.5
Pu-241	4.6	11.5	13.4
Pu-242	1.4	4.5	4.9
Pu-238 + 240 + 242	27.1	31.2	30.9
Spontaneous Fission Rate (Neutrons/sec/gm)	287	363	371

5. For example, the two LWRs promised North Korea in a 1994 U.S.-DPRK agreement were nearly 10 times the size of the indigenous natural uranium reactors they were supposed to replace and therefore had a plutonium production capacity about twice that of the natural uranium reactors.

6. There was an additional cause for alarm and chagrin. India used American heavy water in the reactor that produced the plutonium. The heavy water had been sold under a 1956 contract that restricted its use to "peaceful uses." India claimed its explosion was "peaceful."

7. This is still a common view in nuclear bureaucracies, not least in the U.S. Department of Energy, where it underlies advanced plutonium-fueled reactor and spent fuel reprocess research and development.

8. To cite one important example, Munir Khan, who, as head of the Pakistani Atomic Energy Commission in the 1970s, launched the weapons program and associated fuel cycle activities, studied in the United States on a Fullbright Grant and received an MSc in nuclear engineering from Argonne National Laboratories as part of the Atoms for Peace Program. See www.hipakistan.com/en/detail.php?newsId=en62190&F_catID=17&f_type=source&day=.

9. See Justin T. Long, Engineering for Nuclear Fuel Reprocessing, American Nuclear Society, 1978. This volume of over 1,000 pages was published by the Atomic Energy Commission in 1967 and republished in 1978 for the Department of Energy. The 1967 Forward by Floyd Culler, Assistant Director of the Oak Ridge National Laboratory and one of the foremost experts on reprocessing, states:

This book presents the engineering aspects of the reprocessing of power-reactor fuels. From many diverse sources of information, an attempt has been made to summarize the basic approaches to the engineering of a chemical separation plant. The book does not offer engineering information only; it also reviews the processes most widely used and most of those under development. Particular attention has been given to describing the equipment used in reprocessing fuel. Shielding, criticality control, liquid and gaseous waste disposal, safety, ventilation, fuel-element storage and handling, materials accountability, and maintenance are covered in summary form, and the information given is supplemented by extensive and selected references to reports that are available from the rather specific domain of atomic energy literature. The information is presented in such a way that the book, either as a whole or in part, can be used as a text for instruction in a course on radiochemical course design. The process data and the underlying engineering principles make the book useful either as a textbook or a handbook. . . . We hope, too, that it will serve as a reasonably accurate introduction to reprocessing technology for those who are now entering the field.

10. The IAEA continued in this mode for many years. After the embarrassment of the discoveries after the first Gulf War that Iraq had run a weapons program under the noses of the IAEA inspectors, the Agency carried out important improvements in its mode of operation. In recent years the IAEA has become a first-rate international inspection agency limited principally by what its Board of Governors will permit.

11. The Germans sought to sell the Brazilians a type of enrichment technology that did not offer much promise. The Brazilians later got involved in centrifuge technology and are now constructing a centrifuge enrichment plant that would supply more or less the fuel needs of one of their two reactors. They have been reluctant, however, to allow the IAEA inspectors to see the centrifuges, presumably because the inspectors would then know the source of the technology. The U.S. Government has so far not reacted to this very suspicious and worrisome state of affairs.

12. Perhaps it would be more accurate to say, "was thought to be tightly held," as the industrial spy A. Q. Khan was already delivering to Pakistan centrifuge plans and contractor lists that he had stolen from Urenco while he worked there.

13. Although it now appears that Pakistan may be trying to revive the plant, possibly with Chinese help.

14. Just before the Shah was overthrown in 1979, as part of a reactor sale agreement, Jimmy Carter had agreed to grant Iran "most favored nation" status for reprocessing so that Iran would not be discriminated against when seeking permission to reprocess U.S.-origin fuel. That meant Iran would now have the same right as Japan to reprocess U.S.-enriched power reactor fuel. The Shah left Iran before the negotiations were concluded. See *Nucleonics Week*, January 12, 1978, pp. 2-3; in Daniel Poneman, *Nuclear Power in the Developing World*, George Allen & Unwin: London, 1982, p. 88, at www.nti.org/e_research/profiles/Iran/1825.html.

15. Carter rapidly reversed himself on the issue of Japanese reprocessing of U.S.-supplied fuel (over which the United States had reprocessing control) after his proliferation policy advisor, Gerard Smith, reminded him that World War II

started after the United States cut off Japan's oil supply. In the case of Pakistan's nuclear weapons program, then in its early stages, the United States looked the other way after the Soviet invasion of Afghanistan so as to promote Pakistani help in opposing the Soviets.

16. In spite of the unfavorable economics, support for plutonium recycle continues, including in high places in the current administration as witnessed by comments on this issue in the President's National Energy Plan of May 2000. Such support is based in part on ideology (on the part of nuclear true believers) but mainly on commercial opportunism (on the part of nuclear fuel firms looking for subsidies). Nuclear fuel firms providing reprocessing and plutonium services have discovered that a process does not have to be economical in order to be profitable.

17. That is what Sigvard Eklund, the IAEA Director General, told one of the authors in conversation in 1976. To correct this view, the U.S. Government offered Mr. Eklund a briefing on the subject. At that briefing. his jaw literally dropped when presented with a slide that refuted his earlier view. The new facts had far-reaching implications for the IAEA inspection system.

18. One needs to reemphasize, because it is so frequently forgotten, that the initial rejection of U.S. reprocessing was done by President Ford. But he lost the election a few days after announcing his policy, and so the focus turned to Jimmy Carter.

19. D. E. Ferguson to F. L Culler, Intra-Laboratory Correspondence, Oak Ridge National Laboratory, "Simple, Quick Processing Plant," August 30, 1977, 22 pp. This is the same Mr. Culler whose Forward to a USAEC volume on reprocessing was cited earlier.

20. The diagram appears in the Washington Post, August 4, 2002, to illustrate an article, "Those N. Korean Reactors Light Up Danger Signals," by Victor Gilinsky and Henry Sokolski. The Oak Ridge report does not see the initial mechanical disassembly of the LWR spent fuel as a particularly difficult step. This issue came up in arguments over the risks posed by the two LWRs that the United States had promised North Korea as part of the 1994 Agreed Framework. The State Department insisted that, while North Korea had experience with reprocessing, it would not be able to reprocess LWR fuel because of the difficulty of cutting up the fuel rods, a part of the process with which a high-capacity French commercial plant had difficulty. The Oak Ridge design proposed abrasive saw cutting underwater, and it refers for the details to the 1967 Long volume which has a section on the subject.

21. IAEA 2001 Safeguards Glossary, p. 22, available on the IAEA web site, www.iaea.org.

22. Report by the Comptroller General of the United States, "Quick and Secret Construction of Plutonium Reprocessing Plants: A Way To Nuclear Weapons Proliferation?," EMD-78-104, October 6, 1978. Senator John Glenn, then Chairman of the Subcommittee on Energy, Nuclear Proliferation and Federal Services,

Committee on Government Affairs, and very active on nuclear proliferation issues, made the request. (Throughout, we do not distinguish between the Oak Ridge report and the Oak Ridge memorandum.)

23. The Arms Control and Disarmament Agency (ACDA), the Department of Energy (DOE), the Nuclear Regulatory Commission (NRC), and the Congressional Research Service (CRS). In terms of his knowledge of reprocessing, the most imposing of the 11 individuals consulted was Manson Benedict, Institute Professor Emeritus, Massachusetts Institute of Technology. The CRS review in its entirety was published separately several days later. Warren Donnelly, "A Preliminary Analysis of the ORNL Memorandum on a Crude Nuclear Fuel Reprocessing Plant," November 4, 1977.

24. According to rumor, they served as a conduit for Israeli intelligence.

25. W. G. Sutcliffe and T. J. Trapp, eds., *Extraction and Utility of Reactor-Grade Plutonium for Weapons (U)*, Lawrence Livermore National Laboratory, April 27, 1995. The report is based on briefings given to the National Academy of Sciences' Committee on International Security and Arms Control during its study of the management and disposition of excess weapons plutonium. The full report is classified. The material used here is taken from an unclassified summary.

26. J. P. Hinton, et al., *Proliferation Resistance of Fissile Material Disposition Program (FMDP) Plutonium Disposition Alternatives:* Report of the Proliferation Vulnerability Red Team, Sandia National Laboratories, Report No. SAND97-8201, October 1996, Section 4.1.1.3, "Recovery Process for LWR or MOX Spent Fuel," pp. 4-3 – 4-9. The work was done in the context of assessing the proliferation resistance of various alternatives for the disposition of stocks of weapons-grade plutonium that have been declared excess to national security needs by the United States and Russia.

27. The Phillips design was for spent fuel with an average burnup of 10,000 MWd/t.

28. H. Schneider, et al., "A Study of the Feasibility of a Small Scale Reprocessing Plant for the Dresden Nuclear Power Station," Report IDO-14521, Phillips Petroleum Company, April 28, 1961. Available from the National Technical Information Service (NTIS), Washington, DC.

29. In our judgment, it is not credible that a sub-national group with the type of skills enumerated in the Sandia report could construct and operate even the simplified plants outlined in the Oak Ridge and Sandia reports.

30. In turn, the plutonium-240 absorbs neutrons to form plutonium-241. Plutonium-240 is not fissionable by neutrons in an LWR core but plutonium-241 is.

31. In time, the Atoms for Peace program permitted the U.S. export of large quantities of HEU to fuel foreign research reactors. There was no question about the dangers of HEU as a bomb explosive. As Albert Wohlstetter once said, "The nuclear bureaucracy knew what they were saying about denaturing plutonium was false, so they didn't think it mattered if they exported HEU, too."

32. The author returned from a 1976 European trip and reported to the National Security Council (NSC) staff that the IAEA Director General and his staff believed plutonium from commercial LWR fuel was not usable for weapons, and that the top German officials, then negotiating a nuclear sale to Brazil that involved reprocessing technology, were adamant in this view. They thought that U.S. statements to the contrary were made for commercial, rather than security, reasons. This report to the NSC led to the November 1976 Selden briefings for select top international nuclear figures that included Sir John Hill, head of the UK Atomic Energy Authority; M. Andre Giraud, the head of the French Atomic Energy Commission (CEA); Dr. Eklund, Director General of the IAEA; and Mr. Ryukichi Imai, a senior advisor on nuclear affairs to the Japanese Foreign Ministry. Shortly before this, the author, then a commissioner of the U.S. Nuclear Regulatory Commission, gave a speech at the Massachusetts Institute of Technology in which he said the following: "Of course, when reactor-grade plutonium is used, there may be a penalty in performance that is considerable or insignificant, depending on the weapon design. But whatever we once might have thought, we now know that even simple designs, albeit with some uncertainty in yield, can serve as effective, highly powerful weapons — reliably in the kiloton range." Victor Gilinsky, "Plutonium, Proliferation, and Policy," Remarks given at MIT, November 1, 1976 (NRC Press Release No. S-14-76).

33. See Robert W. Selden, "Reactor Plutonium and Nuclear Explosives," Lawrence Livermore Laboratory, undated slides.

34. See, for example, *Management and Disposition of Excess Weapons Plutonium*, National Academy of Sciences, National Academy Press, Washington, 1994. The Executive Summary, p. 4, states:

> Plutonium of virtually any isotopic composition, however, can be used to make nuclear weapons. Using reactor-grade rather than weapon-grade plutonium would present some complications. But even with relatively simple designs such as that used in the Nagasaki weapon — which are within the capabilities of many nations and possibly some subnational groups — nuclear explosives could be constructed that would be assured of having yields of at least 1 or 2 kilotons. Using more sophisticated designs, reactor-grade plutonium could be used for weapons having considerably higher yields.

A report of a U.S.-Japanese arms control study group arrived at the following statement: "The participants agreed that as a technical matter, with some additional efforts, a country can produce nuclear weapons using any kind of plutonium, using well-known technologies." The members of the working group on reactor-grade plutonium included Hiroyoshi Kurihara, former Executive Director of the Japanese Power Reactor and Nuclear Fuel Development Corporation; Atsuyuki Suzuki, Professor of Nuclear Engineering at the University of Tokyo; and Victor Gilinsky. The overall report was published as Next Steps in Arms Control and Non-Proliferation, Carnegie Endowment for International Peace, 1996. See also

Richard L. Garwin, "Reactor-Grade Plutonium Can be Used to Make Powerful and Reliable Nuclear Weapons: Separated Plutonium in the Fuel-Cycle Must Be Protected As If It Were Nuclear Weapons," August 26, 1998, available on www.fas.org.

35. In nearly 200 fuel assemblies containing over 40,000 fuel rods.

36. There is an exception worth noting. Some fuel is removed early from a reactor, generally because it is not performing properly, possibly because it is leaking radioactive material. The plutonium is such a fuel and will have a composition higher in plutonium-239 than the fuel that remains in the reactor longer.

37. The details come from a chart, "Trends in LWR Pu Production," in a set of briefing slides, Light-Water Reactor Fueling Handling and Spent Fuel Characteristics, J.A. Hassberger, Lawrence Livermore National Laboratory, February 26, 1999. The briefing was presented to a Stanford University/Livermore Laboratory group preparing a report on the problems of safeguarding the LWRs to be supplied to North Korea under the 1994 U.S.-DPRK Agreed Framework, "Verifying the Agreed Framework," Michael May, General Editor, UCRL-ID-142936/CGSR-2001-001, April 2001.

38. The distinction is made in a useful paper by Bruno Pellaud, a former deputy director general of the IAEA and head of the IAEA Department of Safeguards. Bruno Pellaud, "Proliferation Aspects of Plutonium Recycling," *Journal of Nuclear Materials Management*, Fall 2002, Volume XXXI, No. 1, p. 30. He provides the following table:

Grades	Pu-240	Usability
Super grade (SG)	<3 percent	Best quality
Weapon grade (WG)	3-7 percent	Standard material
Fuel grade (FG)	7-18 percent	Practically usable
Reactor grade (RG)	18-30 percent	Conceivably usable
MOX grade	>30 percent	Practically unusable

Table. Plutonium Mixtures for Explosive Purposes.

The categories are, to some extent, arbitrary, but they make for useful peg points. Pellaud's aim is obviously to vindicate the use of MOX grade fuel. Still, he makes helpful points along the way.

39. J. Carson Mark, "Reactor Grade Plutonium's Explosive Properties", Nuclear Control Institute, 1990.

40. An initiator is a contrivance that injects neutrons into the device at the proper moment — when the nuclear explosive has been compressed to a super-critical state — to start the explosive chain reaction. If the neutrons arrive too early, we get a reduction in yield, at worst, a fizzle. If the neutrons come too late, there may be no nuclear explosion at all.

CHAPTER 6

COPING WITH BIOLOGICAL THREATS AFTER SARS

Alan P. Zelicoff

The outbreak of an often fatal lung disease, initially called "Severe Acute Respiratory Syndrome" (SARS)[1] took the international public health community by surprise. Denoted with the typical medical nomenclature of a syndrome—a combination of symptoms and signs—SARS occurred at a time of extraordinary tension among public health practitioners. The not-too-distant memories of the anthrax bioterror event in the United States in the fall of 2001 and the rapid downhill course of dozens of SARS victims captured headlines and invited endless speculation as to the source of the SARS illness (natural vs. sinister), its cause (infectious agent vs. toxic chemical), and the real rate of growth of the epidemic. Because of sketchy reporting from China, the probable initial focus of the outbreak only added to confusion and fear. Travel to China, Southeast Asia, and Singapore plummeted, and passengers disembarking from ships and airplanes from those same areas were screened carefully for respiratory symptoms when they arrived at destinations in the West and Europe. Passengers waiting to board airplanes also were screened carefully, while millions of Chinese and Singaporeans took their own initiatives against the presumed infection by wearing surgical masks and staying out of circulation on crowded streets and public transport. Even into the fall of 2003, some parts of China still were visited infrequently by domestic and international travelers for fear of continuing contagion.

At the time of the writing of this chapter, it is far too soon to enumerate the lessons of the SARS outbreak for national security (and indeed, international security) in a comprehensive way. However, several observations may be instructive to both policy decisionmakers and public health planners.

First, it is abundantly clear that rapid, uncensored information from physicians and hospitals is essential in managing this—or any—infectious disease outbreak, whether it is naturally occurring (as SARS turned out to be) or resulting from bio-terrorism (as initially was feared in the SARS outbreak). There is little question that the "quality" of the information, coming as it does from expert clinicians and infectious disease specialists, is good enough in its raw form to provide "actionable" data. Indeed, once the World Health Organization (WHO) heard from a few isolated clinicians that an apparently severe form of respiratory illness had appeared in just a small handful of patients, it was sufficient to organize teams of epidemiologists and virologists to travel to widely separated parts of the globe to begin to nail down the source of the disease, isolate the causal agent and even divine its mechanism of spread. Transmission of the data in near-real time via the Internet (and with only minimal review and proofing) probably saved tens of thousands of lives in this epidemic.

Second, it is equally clear that a forced *absence* of information in the midst of an outbreak is devastating for individuals and for the local economy. The Chinese government, in particular, actively suppressed the exchange of data internally and shared nothing with foreign or WHO public health officers until embarrassed into doing so by international outcry. No one can doubt any longer the magnification of fear and panic—and thus loss of reason and reasonable behavior of masses of people—when physicians and local public health officials are operating in a scientific vacuum. I return to this point about information in the text of this chapter several times as I think it may be the most important lesson of all from the SARS outbreak of 2003.

Third, even when a severe and novel disease entity emerges, with open flow of information it is possible to effectively "rule out" a biological weapons attack. This lesson is, of course, tenuous, but when the SARS experience is combined with previous outbreaks of mysterious, fatal respiratory disease—such as the Hantavirus pulmonary syndrome in New Mexico in 1991—decisionmakers can take great comfort in the ability of epidemiologic sleuthing to distinguish between nefarious activities and acts of nature. Needless to say, a misstep in the face of *possible* bioterrorism could result in a catastrophe.

Fourth, the tools of modern molecular biology are now so widely spread that it is possible, even easy, for investigators working simultaneously in multiple laboratories to, in effect, independently validate each others' work. In the earliest days of the SARS outbreak, there was some confusion over what organism might be causing the disease. But for the use of gene sequencing in two separate laboratories, this confusion could have undermined an understanding of the source and nature of the pathogen for many weeks. Molecular biology is, unfortunately, a two-edged sword and can certainly be used for illicit purposes, but, in this case, the needed knowledge was discovered swiftly and verified collaboratively. It is hard to overstate the profound power of biological science to do good.

These lessons certainly will affect the response of the public health community to future outbreaks. New outbreaks have always been inevitable, but one could not be nearly so certain about the effectiveness of public health actions. Past successes have been realized much more slowly (for example, with the eradication of smallpox in the wild) or depended on a considerable amount of luck (Hantavirus did not, thank Providence, spread from person-to-person by any route, nor did anthrax in Washington, DC). We will have to do as well in the next outbreak as we did during the SARS epidemic—even better, if our luck runs out, and we face a highly communicable, fatal disease such as a new strain of influenza. I will expand on this requirement more in the text.

While the pathogen responsible for the illness—a novel Coxsackie Virus—seems clear, the economic costs, lives interrupted, and the effectiveness of the public health response still are being tallied. This much appears certain: The virus does not seem to transmit easily as an aerosol as does influenza, but rather as a heavier-than-air droplet that falls onto surfaces or the host's face and hands. These surfaces are then contaminated, and an unwitting individual who touches those surfaces and then touches his nose or mouth provides the transmission mechanism for infection. Had SARS spread by an airborne route, one person coughing or sneezing might well have been able to infect dozens of other people who had no immunity to the virus (and most probably do not). An infectious disease catastrophe might have resulted, reminiscent of the world "pandemic" of influenza in 1918-19 that killed about 10 percent of the world's population, including most prominently young, otherwise healthy adults.

It is not possible to extract the instructive lessons of SARS without some understanding of the fundamental scientific facts. Thus, I will summarize briefly the medical aspects of SARS (including short-term and long-term prognosis in patients) and review the history of the SARS epidemic to date, while highlighting the early dynamics and often frightening spread of the disease. Virologists around the world quickly responded to the need for identification of the pathogen and developed a diagnostic test within a few weeks of the earliest indications of the outbreak — a phenomenal set of accomplishments. Rapid communication of results between several centers in Europe, Asia, and the United States permitted confirmation of laboratory findings; this not only dramatically facilitated an understanding of the fundamental biology of the organism and its interaction with nonimmune human hosts, but also enabled public health officials to define a likely epidemiologic model for the spread of the disease.

I will also speculate as to how the international community might do better when the next new epidemic makes its appearance, as it most assuredly will. Speculation is a dangerous exercise in medicine and biology where rarely, if ever, do the complexities of disease spread fit into compact mathematical expression like the equations of motion in physics, but there is little doubt that the SARS epidemic underscored, yet again, the unfortunate triumph of politics over reason in many aspects of the collaborative management of communicable disease. It seems that high-ranking officials in the Chinese health establishment, and even Chinese government leaders, sought to hide the extent of the epidemic, as they hoped that micro-organisms would respect borders, political decisions, and national sovereignty. Even in the short-run, this was a bankrupt policy. The Chinese economy suffered severe losses — even more than the rest of eastern and southern Asia, struggling to recover from an economic recession made all the worse by the September 11, 2001, terrorist attacks and subsequent war in Afghanistan and the Middle East. After the passage of nearly a year, the full extent of the epidemic on the Chinese mainland was still uncertain, with incomplete accounting of even the total number of victims and their location. The reservoir of origin for the disease remains a mystery.

In addition, I believe that the SARS epidemic is instructive for the arms control community currently debating the utility of monitoring and verification proposals for treaties such as the Biological and

Toxin Weapons Convention (BTWC), and trying to uncover the trail of physical and documentary evidence of the Hussein regime's biological weapons program in Iraq. Here the lessons are not so pleasant. It perhaps is obvious that the illicit, intentional use of a biological weapon, or an accident that might occur in their development, would engender even tighter control of information and greater volume of denials than what we witnessed in China in the early days of the SARS outbreak. That the Chinese government could cover up a serious outbreak for months is sobering; it is much easier to cover up illicit work on biological agents for weapons purposes as the latter occur almost exclusively in laboratories or in other highly controlled facilities.

Tracking disease—especially when the disease causes severe symptoms and spreads in ways not previously seen—is problematic even under the best of circumstances. When there is a deeper political agenda designed to obfuscate the data and deny access to time-sensitive information, the outcome can be disastrous, as might well occur if a state or terrorist organization employed biological weapons. We were fortunate that the SARS agent's mechanism of spread was inefficient, for had transmission been like that of other viral diseases such as measles or influenza, many more people would have died for lack of easily obtained pieces of data, let alone the enormous strain on limited medical resources such as intensive-care unit beds that were needed to save the lives of the most ill patients. We will not necessarily be so lucky the next time.

Medical Aspects of SARS: Diagnosis, Treatment and Outcome.

As of early August 2003, WHO reported[2] that there had been approximately 8,500 cases of SARS in 32 countries and territories. The median age of SARS patients was about 40 years (although patients as young as 1 and as old as 90 have been confirmed as SARS victims). About 20 percent of patients were health-care workers, indicating that, despite reasonable precautions from the outset of the epidemic, close contact with patients confers a high risk for transmission. SARS has a high mortality: about 11 percent of patients die. More than half of the currently known SARS cases are from China where reporting remains incomplete; there will probably be more patients among survivors of SARS in China, and certainly among those who have died in recent months. We now know that older patients fare badly, as about 45 percent of all patients over age 60 die. The combination of advanced age, intensive care unit (ICU) admission, and the need for mechanical ventilation is associated with an 80 percent mortality rate.

WHO believes that the first case of SARS occurred in November 2002 in southeastern China, some 2 months before the first case occurred outside of the country — as it happens, in the United States on January 9, 2003. The vast majority of nonmainland Chinese cases have occurred in just four countries or territories: Hong Kong (now a Special Administrative Region of China), Taiwan, Singapore, and Canada accounting for approximately 3,000 cases. In the United States, there have been 33 cases of SARS, though it should be noted that, because of the similarities between SARS and other causes of acute respiratory illness, the diagnosis of some of the initial "suspected SARS" cases, will doubtless turn out to have been due to other causes, both infectious and noninfectious.

Medical school professors are fond of saying that "the human body has only so many ways of responding to assault from toxic or infectious agents." What they mean is that the symptoms that patients experience — including severe symptoms such as shortness of breath and high fever — can be caused by a large number of agents. Indeed, SARS initially begins like most respiratory viruses with fever, dry cough, muscle aches, and headache. The changes in the levels of white blood cells mirrors those of influenza and even the common cold virus. SARS is one more in a long list of "flu-like" illnesses, but the emerging picture is one of much higher than "flu-like" mortality. Fortunately, as already noted, SARS is much harder to transmit and catch than influenza.

A large series of SARS patients from Canada — the country with the most SARS cases outside of Asia — points to the severity of the clinical disease.[3] About one out of five SARS victims are admitted to an ICU, and almost all of these patients require mechanical ventilation due to respiratory failure, with low blood oxygen saturation, severe fatigue from increased work of respiration, and accumulation of large amounts fluid in the air sacs (alveoli) of the lungs. Significantly, half of the mechanically ventilated patients die despite the most advanced care. Thus, when respiratory failure occurs in SARS, it is an ominous prognostic indicator. A similar experience has been reported from Singapore.[4]

SARS, then, is best thought of as one form of Adult Respiratory Distress Syndrome (ARDS), defined as a clinical condition in which there is shortness of breath, abnormal findings in chest x-ray, and low oxygen levels in the blood. ARDS usually is associated with injury to the lung and may be preceded by a variety of contributory actors including trauma, infection, and shock, among many others. The mechanisms leading to ARDS in patients with otherwise uncomplicated infection from the SARS virus or other micro-organisms remain obscure. Whatever the underlying cause of disturbance of normal lung function, all cases of ARDS necessitate ICU management. Treatment is supportive, meaning that patients are provided with oxygen, fluids, nutrition via gastric tubes or intravenously, and aggressive respiratory toilet, while one hopes for the lung physiology to return to normal.

At autopsy, microscopic examination of the lung shows fluid accumulation in the alveolar sacs, loss of the normal cilia of the bronchial tubes that clear secretions from the lungs, and occasionally secondary bacterial pneumonia.[5] Interestingly, at the time of death, little or no virus is identified in the lung, even in the most severely affected portions of the organ. However, antibodies against Coronavirus almost always are found in the bloodstream, indicating a recent infection with this organism. The absence of organisms is not unusual. When influenza leads to ARDS (as it does on very rare occasion), it is the rule that the virus can not be recovered or grown from lung tissue.

The organism believed to be causal in most cases of SARS is a variety of Coronavirus (officially, "SARS-associated Coronavirus" [SARS-CoV]). It was identified by a remarkable collaboration among scientists from Vietnam, Hong Kong, Taiwan, Thailand, and the United States[6] and simultaneously by investigators in Germany, France, and the Netherlands.[7] It is probably fair to say that never before has a previously unrecognized disease been characterized so quickly, and against the current of mainstream virologic thought. Coronavirses have been well-described as the cause of illness in humans, but never had there been fatalities from this viral family. About one-third of all cases of the common cold are caused by the Coronavirus, and it also occasionally may cause diarrhea in young children. Death from Coronavirus sub-types was unknown.

The isolation of the organism led almost immediately to a diagnostic test based on the presence of antibodies in patients who were recovering from the illness, which was invaluable for broad population studies to establish the means of transmission, as well as the overall susceptibility to and incidence of the disease. In some cases, the antibody test also could be used to make the diagnosis of SARS when it was unclear if the patient was suffering from the Coronavirus or not.

Currently, there is little information on the value of anti-viral drugs, even though it appears that the SARS-CoV is sensitive to ribavarin (a well known anti-microbial agent) in tissue culture. Based on all of the clinical studies published to date, there is almost no evidence that treatment with ribavirin alters the outcome of patients with SARS. This, too, is not unusual for virus-caused diseases, although it may be that in the known cases of SARS, the diagnosis was made after a narrow therapeutic window—between the time of initial infection and onset of the most severe symptoms—had passed. In addition, it is possible that the respiratory failure relates to an individual host's immune system response to the virus rather than to the damage caused by the infection itself.

Because there has been limited time to follow SARS survivors, it is not known if chronic lung problems will plague these patients. However, in ARDS from other causes, patients who have been ventilated mechanically have been shown to have residual functional abnormalities[8] and a generally poor quality of life[9] for many months after hospital discharge. It is unlikely that the experience of survivors of SARS will be much different.

Compared to influenza A and each of its subtypes, SARS-CoV is a highly mortal disease. However, because of the much higher prevalence of influenza worldwide and in the United States, the number of deaths attributed to influenza is many times that of SARS. Between 1976 and 1997, the Center for Disease Control in the

United States estimates that, on average, more than 50,000 people died each year, and influenza is estimated to be involved (either as a direct cause of death or contributing to death in patients with other ailments) in a bit more than 2 percent of all deaths. In 1996, about 14,000 people in the United States died as a direct result of influenza, and another 54,000 with chronic circulatory or respiratory disease died from complications of influenza. It is difficult to know the overall mortality rate from influenza as statistics on the incidence of the disease are not available, but it is probably less than 1 percent. As with SARS, patients over age 65 have the highest mortality among age groups.

Finally, it is likely that SARS has been under diagnosed, with many mildly symptomatic individuals unrecognized. WHO criteria for SARS have been shown to be very specific (that is, resulting in few false positives) but not very sensitive (that is, a large number of false negatives).[10] Future population-based serologic surveys may define the actual incidence of the disease. For now, our description of SARS illness is largely limited to the population that is sick enough to seek medical care.

Thus, SARS-CoV is a significant cause of morbidity but, in total, has involved a tiny fraction of the number of people who contract influenza in any given year. The mortality from SARS in those infected is much higher than influenza, but because of the millions of infections with influenza every year in the United States alone, the number of deaths from influenza exceed those from SARS by at least three or four orders of magnitude.

SARS: History, Epidemiology, and Isolation of Causal Organism.

It is now reasonably certain that the first cases of SARS occurred in early November 2002 in Guangdong Province in southeastern China (see Map 1). The patient was a businessman, but the significance of his disease was recognized only in retrospect, and his illness, along with those of hundreds of other individuals with the same severe respiratory symptoms in the same province, was unknown outside China for some months. By early 2003, there were four major foci of life-threatening respiratory disease beyond mainland China: Hong Kong, Vietnam, Singapore, and Canada (Toronto).

Map 1.

It is not yet clear how many people in Guangdong the businessman infected in November 2002. The first patient outside of China to become ill with SARS was a 64-year-old physician from Guangdong Province who became symptomatic while visiting relatives in Hong Kong (now commonly referred to as the Hong Kong Special Administrative Region of China).[11] When he arrived in Hong Kong on February 21, 2003, he had been mildly ill for about 5 days, but felt well enough to go sightseeing and shopping with relatives.[12] He was admitted to the hospital the following day. About 3 days later, a 53-year-old male who accompanied the physician on his excursion around Hong Kong then became ill, and he was hospitalized 2 days later on February 26. Over the next 17 days, eight other people became ill with identical symptoms, all of them either staying at the same hotel as the physician index case, or who had contact with him in the hospital or with other patients with respiratory disease recently hospitalized.

At about the same time, on February 28, a patient presented to the Vietnamese French Hospital of Hanoi with an influenza-like illness. Because of recent small outbreaks over the past 2 years in Southeast Asia of influenza transmitted directly from humans to birds, physicians in Hanoi became concerned that they were seeing another similar outbreak. Mortality in previous human avian influenza ("bird flu") cases was extremely high, and because of the fear that avian influenza had once again jumped into humans, WHO was contacted. Dr. Carlo Urbani, an infectious disease expert, was dispatched, and, within a few days, he and a small team of virologists and epidemiologists arrived in Hanoi. With in a few weeks, Dr. Urbani and at least five other health care workers would also be dead, all from the mysterious new disease contracted from patients they cared for.

Urbani and his colleagues set to work immediately collecting specimens, reviewing patient histories, and assisting hospital workers with infection control and patient isolation procedures. By March 9—just 10 days after the first patient in Vietnam appeared at the French Hospital—WHO was worried enough by Dr. Urbani's data to request an emergency meeting with high ranking health ministers in Hanoi, and recommended strict enforcement of patient isolation and barrier protection for all healthcare workers in Hanoi hospitals caring for patients with respiratory symptoms. *Medecins sans Frontiers* (Doctors without Borders), an international medical aid agency, provided additional physicians and personal protective equipment. More infection control specialists were dispatched to Hanoi.

Also on March 9, a 32-year-old Singaporean physician became ill with a high fever while in New York City on a visit. The previous week while in Singapore, he had cared for a patient from Hong Kong who presented "atypical pneumonia" on March 3. Four days later the doctor developed a dry cough and a rash. On March 16, while in Frankfurt on his way back to Singapore, he became so short of breath that he was sent to Frankfurt University Hospital and was admitted to the ICU. Subsequently, two people in close contact with this physician—his wife and his mother—became ill about the time the doctor was admitted to the hospital.

Unknown to physicians in Hong Kong, Singapore, and Frankfurt, on February 25, 2003, in Toronto, Canada, a 78-year-old woman developed fever, sore throat, and a dry cough 2 days after returning from a 10-day visit to Hong Kong. She was given an oral anti-bacterial antibiotic but became progressively more ill. She died on March 5 while at home. Her 43-year-old son became ill with symptoms essentially identical to those of his mother on February 27, and on March 2 was admitted to the hospital. Progressive respiratory difficulties supervened, and he was placed on a mechanical ventilator on March 3. Despite careful intensive treatment, he died on March 13, roughly 2 weeks after becoming ill. An autopsy was performed, which revealed changes typical of the Adult Respiratory Distress Syndrome, but no evidence of viral infection was identified.[13]

By the end of March, there would be more than 100 cases of SARS in Canada, 156 in Hong Kong, and at least 40 in Vietnam. Many other countries would go on to identify cases of what became known as SARS within weeks. But, there was little, if any, information forthcoming from China. The Chinese government reported 305 cases of "atypical pneumonia" with at least five deaths to WHO on February 11, 2003 (even though an unusual disease outbreak had first been recognized in November 2002), but initially the disease was attributed to a rare cause of pneumonia, Chlamydia pneumonae.

WHO first alerted public health officials to the presence of a "severe form of pneumonia" on March 12, 2003,[14] after connecting the illnesses described above. A case definition was established and promulgated via the Internet and WHO bulletins. This case definition consisted of a set of symptoms (patient complaints) and signs (physicians' findings at the time of physical examination and also laboratory tests and X-ray results). The combination of signs and symptoms—a "syndrome"—is not to be confused with a diagnosis based on a specific, known cause (such as an infectious organism) and was called "Severe Acute Respiratory Syndrome" (SARS).

The first summary of the epidemiology of SARS—the patterns of disease by age, sex, and travel history of victims—appeared on March 31, published on the Web page of the *New England Journal of*

Medicine (NEJM). Never before had information about a completely new syndrome been categorized, collated, analyzed, checked, and distributed so quickly, nor had multicountry peer review ever before been marshaled so expeditiously. NEJM has an international reputation for high standards, and its requirements for publication, even in electronic form, are as stringent as any scientific journal anywhere in the world.

Then, remarkably on March 24, scientists at the CDC working closing with researchers in Hong Kong isolated and identified a virus of the family of viruses called Coronavirus (CoV) from the first patients with SARS (see Figure 1). They had taken respiratory secretions, blood samples, and other body fluids from SARS victims and plated the material out on a wide variety of animal cells growing in tissue culture vats. Within a few days of starting these experiments, investigators noted that in one particular cell culture — monkey kidney cells — were dying. Inspection of the cells under the electron microscope showed that they were filled with viral particles.

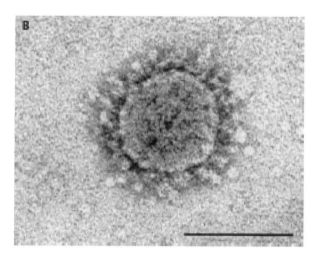

Figure 1: Coronavirus Urbani as Seen in the Electron Microscope (NEJM 348: 1954-66, 2003).

Within a week, a key portion of the genome of CoV had been completely sequenced and compared with all other known Coronavirus strains. It was found to be different not only from all other strains of Coronavirus that cause disease in humans, but from those strains that cause disease in a multitude of animal species: birds, cattle, pigs, and cats (both wild and domesticated). A group of investigators in Germany did the same, and proved that their gene sequencing was completely consistent with the CDC-Hong Kong group. Their results, along with a detailed description of clinical and autopsy findings, laboratory studies, and even a highly-specific prototype antibody test were described and published on the New England Journal web site on April 10, less than 7 weeks after the first cases of SARS appeared in Canada and Hong Kong. In honor of Dr. Urbani, the proposed name of the novel Coronavirus is the "Urbani strain of SARS-associated coronavirus).

How Do We Know That *C. Urbani* Causes SARS?

In response to any infection, mammalian immune systems produce a panoply of responses. At least a dozen different cells capture and degrade the invading organism, and some of these cells engulf and kill the virus directly. Other cells dismember the outer membrane constituents of the virus and deliver selected pieces to other cells that, after the passage of a few days, begin to generate antibodies that bind more-or-less specifically to the infectious agent. The quantity (called "titer") of antibodies (of several subtypes) slowly rises, usually over the course of 3 to 8 weeks. The presence and quantity of these antibodies can be identified by using antibodies from other animals (goats are a typical source) that bind to *human* antibodies — caprine anti-human antibodies — that are tagged further with fluorescent markers. If human anti-Coronavirus antibodies are obtained from an individual patient's blood and exposed to cells on a microscope slide containing the offending viral particles growing in them, the antibodies will bind to the cells. When the tagged caprine anti-human antibodies then are applied to the microscope slide, the cells become dotted with brightly fluorescing material (easily seen when illuminated with ultraviolet light source) and quantified. This process is called "indirect-immunoflourescence," so named because the binding of the patient's own antibodies against the infectious agent is seen "indirectly" via the fluorescence of the tagged antibodies that, in turn, are bound tightly to target sites on the virus on a microscope slide, rather than by visualizing the antibodies themselves (which are too small to be seen with ordinary microscopes).

The case for Coronavirus *Urbani* as the cause of SARS was capped with the demonstration of increasing titer of antibodies in patients who recovered from SARS during 3 or 4 weeks of convalescence *and* a survey of hundreds of old (pre-SARS) blood-bank samples that failed to reveal any antibodies against C. *Urbani*. Thus, not only were patients who recovered from SARS generating specific antibodies to the virus, the virus had to be novel for, if it were ever in circulation previously in the human population, at least some blood donors would be expected to show evidence of past infection.

To date, Coronavirus *Urbani* has been found in respiratory secretions and fecal matter, but rarely in the bloodstream of patients suffering with disease. In animals, various strains of Coronavirus are isolated from the same sources. Most virologists believe that all of these materials are infectious.

Origin of Coronavirus Strain Urbani.

The family of Coronavirus is known to mutate frequently, that is, the genome of the virus may change suddenly, resulting in a new species of Coronavirus that may have a different host range or result in more severe disease. One way this mutation can occur is via the process of *recombination*, wherein two (or perhaps more) Coronavirus species that happen to infect a given animal at the same time shuffle and exchange their DNA within animal host cells. The daughter virus types that emerge from the animal cell then may contain an entirely new DNA construct (or, multiple types may result each with a unique and novel genome). A similar process occurs from time to time with the influenza virus, and when it does, a never-before seen strain of the virus may begin to circulate in the population. In addition, close and repeated contact between animals that carry these reassorted strains of influenza and humans — as occurs often in crowded live-animal markets in Asia and on farms—seems to create a perfect niche for the passage of novel influenza strain to humans. It is not surprising that new varieties of influenza in recent decades have first appeared in Asia, particularly in China and Hong Kong.

Since Coronavirus species are the cause of a multitude of animal diseases (usually presenting as fatal respiratory disease or dehydration from diarrhea), and since agricultural animals tend to live in close quarters, spread from animal to animal is the rule, thereby permitting enormous numbers of reassortment variants.[15] Human farmers or customers in crowded animal markets are potential targets for novel strains that may have surprising changes in their host range. All of the known human Coronavirus species characterized to date cause mild illnesses: about 30 percent of "colds" (technically upper respiratory infections, not involving the lungs or interfering with respiration) are caused by a Coronavirus. On rare occasion, mild diarrhea in humans also results from Coronavirus.

Thus, it appears that an unwitting human in southern China acquired a novel strain of Coronavirus sometime in the fall of 2002. The source has not been identified yet. Some virologists believe that the organism was transmitted to humans from the civet cat, a gastronomic delicacy in China. However, human consumption of this animal, a 5,000 year tradition in China, casts doubt on the civet as the primary source of the disease;[16] nonetheless, Chinese officials banned the sale of wild animals in Guangdong. Dr. David Heyman, WHO's executive director for communicable disease, cautioned that the source of the virus remains speculative, and that it is possible that a seasonal pattern may emerge over time, suggesting environmental niches that might provide alternative paths of transmission beyond consumption of wild animals[17] or direct contact with Coronavirus-infected humans.

Transmission and Response:
Should SARS Have Caused such a Fuss?

In the early stages of a disease outbreak involving a manifestly novel agent, many uncertainties arise in predicting the speed of transmission of disease. As with SARS, the mode of transmission is not immediately apparent early in many epidemics. Among the questions that epidemiologists try to answer are:

- Are there animal and/or insect vectors?
- Do infected individuals spread the micro-organism via aerosolization during coughing or sneezing? If individuals are infectious to others, how long do they remain so?
- What is the rate of new cases (sometimes called the "incidence") of disease?
- Are quarantine and travel restrictions necessary?

After establishing a "case definition," the primary data that public health officials need to answer these questions comes from the simple reporting of the time of onset of each case, location of the individual, and demographic information such as sex, approximate age, recent travel, and perhaps the individual's employment. With statistical tests to determine the degree of confidence in the data, epidemiologists can plot the data in a variety of ways to determine trends and thus infer the "behavior" of the epidemic. Needless to say, in the absence of routine information flow — as occurred in mainland China — even this simple analysis is impossible.

In March and April 2003, during the first few weeks of the SARS epidemic outside of mainland China, reporting was timely and generally complete. Although the media tended to focus on the fear (even panic) attendant to the unknown cause of the syndrome, it was possible to discern that the epidemic was growing slowly, and not at all what one might expect from an influenza-like virus that spread via aerosol from person-to-person. Simply by plotting the total number of reported cases by country over time, a benign picture emerged:[18]

SARS Cases and Deaths

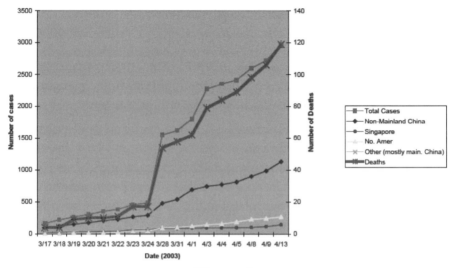

Figure 2.

Note that, the China mainland aside, the growth in the number of cases is approximately linear. Indeed, using basic statistical tools, it was possible to postulate a linear growth model, and test this hypothesis against actual number of cases:

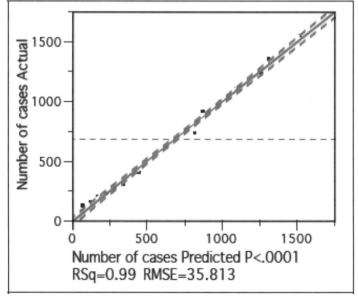

Figure 3.

Influenza (or closely related virus strains) almost certainly would have caused an exponential increase in the number of cases. As the epidemic proceeded and more cases were reported, public health personnel increasingly were confident that spread of the virus depended on close contact with infected individuals or contaminated surfaces.

With the exception of mainland China, exchange of data in the SARS epidemic was unprecedented.

Early Lessons from the SARS Epidemic for Public Health and Counterterrorism.

The tools of molecular biology, epidemiology with contact tracing, and modern communications via the Internet resulted in an unprecedented public health triumph: Within a few days of the first cases, WHO was able to organize collaborating teams of virologists, epidemiologists, and infectious disease experts, each critical to the isolation, identification, and containment of the disease. That the organism responsible for SARS was never before described underscores the profound importance of the global response and the value of independent groups working simultaneously. Indeed, the contemporaneous sequencing of the viral genome in the United States and Germany provided at once the identification of the organism and verification thereof. Further, the results along with expert interpretation in the context of the epidemic were communicated worldwide within days. As has been noted by others, if "business as usual" had applied in SARS, we might still be trying to identify the causal organism, and the disease might have been much more widely spread.

At the same time, the response to SARS might have been quicker — with fewer attendant deaths and fewer cases — had international public health workers been aware of the "atypical pneumonia" cases in China that began in November 2002. More than ever before, the management of novel infectious disease outbreaks is highly dependent on timely information. Transportation and commerce virtually assure that microbial pathogens in one part of the globe will be in major transport hubs within days or even hours, increasing the likelihood of multipoint outbreaks and adding to the bewilderment of infectious disease experts trying to unravel the origin and modes of spread of the agent. The key, of course, is open dissemination of information; it appears that the Chinese public health infrastructure failed to do its part in what we now know to be the first days of SARS-CoV. Indeed, it was not until July 2005 that Chinese investigators published substantive information on their experience with SARS,[19] when an entire issue of the most widely read Chinese medical journal was devoted to SARS. An editorial accompanying the scientific papers mentioned nothing about reporting delays nor interrupted information flow as contributors to both domestic and international spread of SARS.

The ingress of human activity into previously unexplored regions and the close contact between humans and hundreds of animal species guarantees the exchange of countless organisms. Mercifully, most of them will not result in disease (in either humans or animals).

SARS is but the latest in a series of "emerging" diseases—illnesses due to infectious agents that were not described previously—that have begun to affect humans. In just the past few decades, medical journals and newspaper headlines have been filled with articles about these new disease entities: Ebola hemorrhagic fever (from squirrels and perhaps monkeys), Hantavirus Pulmonary Syndrome (from mice), Spongioform encephalopathy (from cows), and monkeypox (transmitted by prairie dogs), all occurring in people. Although this list is incomplete and doubtless other novel diseases await us, similarities can be identified readily. All of the organisms originate in nonhuman species and have occurred when humans and the natural animal hosts come in close contact (indeed, in the case of both Ebola and Spongioform encephalopathy, consumption of infected animal tissue seems to be required). Each of the organisms causes diseases with high mortality (in the case of Ebola and Spongioform encephalopathy, nearly 100 percent), and none can be treated successfully yet. Finally, while treatment is elusive, prevention generally is simple, with either avoidance of contact or, in the case of SARS-CoV, careful isolation of infectious patients until their disease resolves.

Given the characteristics of emerging disease pathogens, rapid identification of disease foci is essential. Remarkably enough, having a pathogen in hand (or surrogate diagnostic test results) is not necessary in order to recognize that a problem may be brewing. Syndrome-based surveillance (SBS), depending only on the signs and symptoms in seriously ill people or animals, may be sufficient to mobilize international action — first with quarantine, followed by the application of new techniques in genomics, molecular biology, immunology and cell culture to identify causal organisms *combined with* the sharing of results so that they may be independently verified. The power of SBS to give early warning to public health officials and government decisionmakers has been described recently,[20] and at least two systems, ESSENCE II and the Syndrome Reporting Information System (SYRIS),[21] have been in operation in several U.S. states for the past 2 years,[22] and SYRIS has been used in Singapore to help manage the SARS epidemic there. Each system draws on the basic tenants of epidemiology: establishing what *kind* of illness a patient (or animal) has; *when* the illness began; and *where* the patient is located or has traveled.

Approaches to SBS fall into two broad categories: "passive" systems that utilize data commonly gathered in the care of patients such as emergency room records, ambulance flowsheets, and even billing from physician offices; and "active" systems that depend on health care providers to identify the case and describe the signs and symptoms observed. There are advantages and disadvantages to each. Passive systems are nonspecific, depend on availability of sensitive patient data via electronic means, and assume that the kind of information cataloged in western medical systems is similar to that gathered elsewhere. Analysis therefore may be difficult, and false alarms may occur. However, passive systems do not require specific input from busy healthcare providers; clerks or administrators (and automated billing systems) can provide much of the needed data.

Active systems exploit physician judgment, depending on doctors to enter required information (preferably via a computer interface with immediate dissemination of reports). In any surveillance system, there is a trade-off between the *quantity* of data and its *quality*, often referred to as the "signal to noise" ratio in scientific disciplines. Active systems operate on the hypothesis that physician are able to determine quickly the severity of illness, even though the underlying etiology is unknown. It may be the case that nonspecific indicators —

such as the raw number of patients ill with mild symptoms (generally not captured in billing statements or "chief complaints" recorded by nursing or ambulance personnel)—will lead to false alarms, triggering costly investigations or preventive measures that are unwarranted. On the other hand, the sudden appearance of even a small number of patients with severe constitutional symptoms (high fever and prostration, for example), along with certain clinical signs such as rash or pneumonia, may be indicative of the earliest stages of an epidemic, including one caused by terrorist use of biological weapons.[23]

Active and passive surveillance systems have not demonstrated their cost-effectiveness yet. However, in at least one important case, syndrome surveillance enabled public health officials to determine rapidly that a report of stolen samples of virulent plague organisms from a medical school in Texas was a hoax.[24] By noting the *absence* of respiratory disease at a time when a high incidence of seasonally-related respiratory symptoms was expected, local officials could assure physicians and the public that there was no reason for worry. In addition, public health officials used the syndrome surveillance system to communicate new information and all-important diagnostic criteria for plague to physicians in the community who, by and large, had never seen a case of this disease.

Conclusions.

The management of the SARS-CoV epidemic of 2003 was, for the most part, a victory for scientists working in epidemiology and molecular biology. Within weeks, the organism was isolated and identified, and a diagnostic test was perfected. Perhaps more important, by careful reporting and contact tracing, it was possible to determine that the disease spread slowly, implying that there was little likelihood of aerosol transmission from person-to-person, a key discovery that changed travel recommendations and even trade dramatically.[25] While there is no question that there were serious economic consequences from the epidemic and nearly 1000 people have died to date, the impact would have been much more severe in the presence of greater uncertainty about the behavior of the virus and the disease it caused.

114

SARS provides decisionmakers and public health officials with a model that generates valuable lessons for the response to future disease outbreaks, including those that are introduced intentionally into the human or animal population by terrorists. The key to the successful management of SARS was the rapid sharing of information. Countries that openly reported information benefited both themselves and other nations. Mortality, though substantial, was modest when compared to the yearly toll from influenza, and economic catastrophe via draconian travel and trade restrictions was avoided.

The international community may be poised to adopt a formal system of routine data sharing via the Internet, overcoming the time delays inherent in traditional reporting hierarchies. Several promising Internet-based applications operating in the United States, Europe, and Asia can provide invaluable information to public health officials trying to limit the spread of infection and to the physicians who care for those who become ill during epidemics. A modest amount of political will is all that is required. Since infectious disease respects no border, people living in countries whose leaders choose to suppress information or subvert open reporting may suffer immeasurably in future outbreaks that are certain to occur.

ENDNOTES - CHAPTER 6

1. I will use the abbreviation "SARS" when referring to the syndrome and SARS-CoV when discussing the disease caused by the newly discovered Coronavirus. More detail is provided in the text.

2. See *www.who.int/csr/sars/country/2003_08_15/en/*.

3. R. A. Fowler, S. E. Lapinsky, D. Hallett, A. S. Detsky, W. J. Sibbald, A. S. Slutsky, and T. E. Stewart, "Critically Ill Patients with Severe Acute Respiratory Syndrome," *Journal Of The American Medical Association* (JAMA), Vol. 290, No. 3, July 16, 2003, pp. 367-373.

4. T. W. K. Lew, T. K. Kwek, D. Tai, A. Earnest, S. Loo, K. Singh, K. M. Kwan, Y Chan, C. F. Yim, S. L. Bek, A. C. Kor, W. S. Yap, Y. R. Chelliah, Y. C. Lai, and S. K. Goh, *idem.*, pp. 374-380.

5. J. M. Nicholls, L. L. M. Poon, K. C. Lee, W. F. Ng, S. T. Lai, C. Y. Leung, C. M. Chu, P. K. Hui, K. L. Mak, W. Lim, K. W. Yan, K. H. Chan, N. C. Tsang, Y Guan, K. Y. Yuen, and J. S. M. Peiris, "Lung Pathology of Fatal Severe Acute Respiratory Syndrome," *Lancet*, Vol. 361, No. 9371, May 24, 2003; pp.1773-1778.

6. Christian Drosten, Stephan Gunther, Wolfgang Preiser, Sylvie van der Werf, Hans-Reinhard Brodt, Stephan Becker, Holger Rabenau, Marcus Panning, Larissa Kolesnikova, Ron A. M. Fouchier, Annemarie Berger, *et al.*, "Identification of a Novel Coronavirus in Patients with Severe Acute Respiratory Syndrome," *New England Journal of Medicine*, Vol. 348, 2003, pp. 1967-1976.

7. Thomas G. Ksiazek, Dean Erdman, Cynthia S. Goldsmith, Sherif R. Zaki, Teresa Peret, Shannon Emery, Suziang Tong, Carlo Urbani, James A. Comer, Wilina Lim, Pierre E. Rollin, Dowell, *et al.*, the SARS Working Group, "A Novel Coronavirus Associated with Severe Acute Respiratory Syndrome," *ibid.*, pp 1953-1966.

8. T. A. Neff, R. Stocker, H. R. Frey, S. Stein, and E. W. Russi, "Long-term Assessment of Lung Function in Survivors of Severe ARDS, *Chest*, Vol. 123, No. 3, March 2003, pp. 845-853.

9. G. Schelling, C. Stoll, C. Vogelmeier, T. Hummel, J. Behr, H. P. Kapfhammer, H. B. Rothenhausler, M. Haller, K. Durst, T. Krauseneck, and J. Briegel, "Pulmonary Function and Health-Related Quality of Life in a Sample of Long-term Survivors of the Acute Respiratory Distress Syndrome," *Intensive Care Medicine*, Vol. 26, No. 9, September 2000, pp. 1304-1311.

10. T. H. Rainer, P. A. Cameron, D. Smit, K. L. Ong, A. N. W. Hung, D. C. P. Nin, A. T. Ahuja, L. C. Y. Si, and J. J. Y. Sung, "Evaluation of WHO Criteria for Identifying Patients with Severe Acute Respiratory Syndrome Out of Hospital: Prospective Observational Study," *British Medical Journal*, Vol. 326, No. 7403, June 21, 2003, pp. 1354-1358.

11. R. P. Wenzel, and M. B. Edmond, *New England Journal of Medicine*, Vol. 348, 2003, pp. 1947-1949.

12. K. W. Tsang, P. L. Ho, G. C. Ooi, *et al.*, "Cluster of Cases of Severe Acute Respiratory Syndrome in Hong Kong," *New England Journal of Medicine*, Vol. 348, 2003, pp. 1977-1985.

13. S. M. Poutanen, D. E. Low, Henry B., S. Finkelstein, *et al.*, "Identification of Severe Acute Respiratory Syndrome in Canada," *New England Journal of Medicine*, Vol. 348, 2003, pp. 1995-2005.

14. See *www.who.int/csr/sars/archive/2003_03_12/en/*. The WHO on-line archives serve as the single most comprehensive source of information about SARS.

15. It is believed that the vast majority of recombinant strains of virus are nonviable because their DNA does not contain the necessary codes to produce functioning daughter virus particles.

16. *British Medical Journal*, Vol. 326, June 7, 2003, p. 1232.

17. *Ibid.*, June 21, 2003, p. 1350.

18. The graphs are taken from an informal paper that I circulated among public health officials in Switzerland, the United States, and Singapore, updated twice weekly in the early weeks of the SARS outbreak. This work was not peer-reviewed, but was reported in *Science*, Vol. 300, April 25, 2003, pp. 558-559.

19. The June 2003 issue of the *Chinese Medical Journal* (Vol. 116, No. 7) and the July 2003 *Chinese Science Bulletin* (Vol 48, No. 13) contain the first publications authored in the People's Republic of China, not including the Hong Kong SAR.

20. M. D. Lewis, J. A. Pavlin, J. L. Mansfield, S. O'Brien, L. G. Boomsma, Y. Elbert, and P. W. Kelley, "Disease Outbreak Detection System Using Syndromic Data in the Greater Washington, DC, Area," *American Journal Of Preventive Medicine*, Vol. 23, No. 3, October 2002 pp. 180-186.

21. For more information on SYRIS, see *syris,arescorporation.com/demo*.

22. Mary Beth Nierengarten, Larry Lutwick, and Suzanne Lutwick, "Syndrome-Based Surveillance for Clinicians on the Frontlines of Healthcare: Focus on Rapid Diagnosis and Notification," *www.medscape.com/viewprogram/2427*.

23. R. P. Kadlec, A. P. Zelicoff, and A. M. Vrtis, "Biological Weapons Control — Prospects and Implications for the Future," *JAMA*, Vol. 278, No. 5, August 6, 1997, pp. 351-356.

24. Tigi Ward, Lubbock Texas Department of Health (personal communication).

25. Some recent evidence suggests that foodhandlers, caterers and chefs in China were a "high risk group" for acquiring SARS-CoV. This adds further evidence in support of the postulate that animals used as food (including, but not limited to chickens and civet cats) in China are the "source" of SARS-CoV. R. P. Wenzel and M. B. Edmonds, "Listening to SARS: Lesson for Infection Control," *Ann Internal Medicine*, 2003 (in press).

SECTION III.

WHAT CAN BE DONE

CHAPTER 7

NEW MISSILES AND MODELS FOR COOPERATION[1]

Dennis M. Gormley and Richard Speier

NOTE: This chapter, first presented by the authors on March 17, 2003, was reviewed and updated by the authors in January 2006.

THE THREAT

Even though ballistic missiles dominated missile nonproliferation deliberations during the last decade of the 20th century, land-attack cruise missiles (LACMs)—most notably America's *Tomahawk*—figured into no less than seven different military contingencies. The *Tomahawk's* most impressive role was reflected in its widespread use against Iraq during Operation DESERT STORM, when, during the first hours of the air campaign, *Tomahawk* strikes greatly leveraged the subsequent effectiveness of manned aircraft by destroying critical Iraqi air defense and command and control targets. *Tomahawks*, too, figured into a variety of much smaller-scale contingencies, the most controversial of which were the attacks on the al-Shifa pharmaceutical plant in Khartoum, Sudan, and al-Qaeda camps in Afghanistan, in retaliation for the al-Qaeda-sponsored embassy bombings in Africa in August 1998.

Although the al-Shifa pharmaceutical plant attack dominated press scrutiny, the ineffectiveness of cruise missile attacks on Osama bin Laden's Afghan camps generated significant interest in new roles for unarmed and subsequently armed unmanned air vehicles (UAVs) even before the terrorist attacks of September 11, 2001 (9/11). Unarmed UAVs, with their extended loiter capability, could provide surveillance and communications connectivity superior to that of manned aircraft. But armed UAVs could do more. In the aftermath of the terrorist attacks on New York City and the Pentagon, the United States, for the first time, effectively unleashed *Predators* armed with two *Hellfire* missiles for use in Afghanistan, and most prominently, in a pinpoint attack against a top al-Qaeda operative and five companions in Yemen. The notion of combining real-time eyes, by way of several organic surveillance packages, with a weapon allowing for the virtually instantaneous engagement of so-called time-critical targets was powerfully appealing. Assuming that the authorization to fire could be prearranged or achieved quickly, such a combined sensor and weapons-carrying UAV would more than compensate for the limitations of using LACMs launched from great distances hours after acquiring targeting intelligence. Arguably, the armed UAV has become the most prominently featured military instrument in America's first war of the 21st century.

The employment of UAVs promises to make military operations more discriminating in their effects. But, as this trend establishes itself, more ominous possibilities are emerging. UAVs—both armed and unarmed—are growing larger. They are breaching the threshold for the most restrictive international nonproliferation restraints. And civilian applications for UAVs are developing. These trends— combined with the inherent capability of UAVs to deliver nuclear, biological, or chemical payloads—set the stage for a new level of proliferation threats—the very opposite of the discriminating use of force.

The American use of armed *Predators* raises important questions not only about how UAVs will help shape America's current military transformation, but also about the extent to which other countries or terrorist groups might emulate American actions and transform their own unarmed UAVs or small manned aircraft into unmanned weapons-delivery systems or crude terror weapons. Recent inspections in Iraq have uncovered a UAV that reportedly is the system that Secretary of State Colin Powell discussed before the UN Security Council in early February 2003 as having been test flown 500km around a racetrack fully autonomously.[2] Equipped with sprayers that Iraq is known to have tested, such a UAV could have threatened regional targets and conceivably even U.S. ones, were such a vehicle launched from a ship offshore or covertly transported into the United States.

The Strategic Setting.

Although the world's UAV inventory is imprecisely documented, according to one recent study, at least 40 countries produce over 600 different UAVs, nearly 80 percent of which could be flown one-way ranges of over 300 kilometres (km) and many substantially farther.[3] Moreover, a small fraction of the world's inventory of antiship cruise missiles — primarily first-generation models with substantial airframe volume — could be converted into land attack missiles with ranges exceeding 300km. Further, there are inviting loopholes in the Missile Technology Control Regime (MTCR) that permit aerospace firms to sell flight management systems specifically designed to turn small manned aircraft (including kit-built ones) into autonomously guided and armed UAVs. Finally, were a country or terrorist group motivated to develop a crude cruise missile or UAV either on its own or with some foreign assistance, it could readily take advantage of the last decade's quantum leap in dual-use technologies that comprise the chief components of autonomous air-vehicle development. These include satellite navigation and guidance furnished primarily by the USA's Global Positioning System, high-resolution satellite imagery from a growing number of commercial vendors, and digital mapping technologies for mission planning.[4]

Impact of Proliferation on American Military Dominance. Should cruise missiles and armed UAVs spread widely and become a dominant feature of military operations or terrorist activity in the 21st century, the international security consequences could be profound. Ironically, perhaps the most significant impact would rebound on the United States — doubtless the most advanced nation around the globe in developing and exploiting land-attack cruise missiles (LACMs) and UAVs for military benefit. The proliferation of LACMs and UAVs to complement ballistic missiles conceivably could bolster the capacities of America's adversaries to oppose U.S.-led interventions in strategically important ways. LACMs and UAVs could furnish new military leverage, due in significant part to the capacity of cruise missiles (due to their steady horizontal flight pattern, releasing anagent along a line of contamination) to enlarge the effective lethal area of biological attacks by at least a factor of ten over ballistic missiles.[5] In addition, the potentially high accuracy of LACMs suggests that even conventionally armed missiles may be able to inflict significant damage on exposed targets. To envisage such damage, one need only consider the airbases that U.S.-led coalition forces used during Operation DESERT STORM on which aircraft were lined up wingtip-to-wingtip, and large tent cities were left open and vulnerable to missile attack.

Cruise missile and UAV proliferation also are likely to create unwanted dilemmas for American missile defenses. The United States currently spends huge sums to defend against ballistic missile threats. Yet, to the extent that America successfully pursues effective theater and national missile defenses against ballistic missiles, nations, and terrorist groups alike will be strongly motivated to acquire LACMs and armed UAVs. For example, the low cost of some cruise missiles and, especially, small airplanes modified to become UAVs, renders the cost-per-kill arithmetic of missile defense exceedingly unfavorable. For example, each *Patriot PAC-3* missile costs between $2-5 million, which compares unfavorably with either a $200,000 LACM or $50,000-per-copy kit airplanes transformed into armed UAVs.[6] Because both ballistic and cruise missile defenses for theater campaigns currently depend largely on the same high-cost, high-performance interceptors, cruise as well as ballistic missile attacks, especially saturation ones and those delivering weapons of mass destruction (WMD) payloads, will present enormous problems for the defender.

Advanced LACMs that fly low and have low observability to air defense radars will raise the cost of cruise missile defense dramatically.[7] Even seemingly easy to detect armed UAVs could challenge legacy air defense radars, including the Airborne Warning and Control Systems (AWACS) and some ground-based radars. Around 65 percent of the UAVs deployed today are propelled by reciprocating engines, which means that they fly at speeds of less than 80 knots per hour. Yet expensive air defense radars like AWACS intentionally eliminate slow flying targets on or near the ground in order to prevent their data processing and display systems from being overly taxed. Although most ground based air defense radars could probably detect such slow flying systems, the limited radar horizon of ground based radars, combined with the possibly large raid size of a threat, means that interceptor batteries could be overwhelmed quickly, and their expensive missile inventories rapidly depleted. There are no simple or cheap solutions that readily return the advantage to the defender.

Regional Military Imbalances. Potential or actual adversaries of American military dominance are not motivated merely to acquire long range missiles to deter or defeat Western-led military interventions. Regional states, rogues or not, may be equally or primarily driven to pursue missile acquisition for uniquely regional reasons. Thus, regional military balances also could be adversely affected by the spread of LACMs and UAVs. Chinese acquisition of M-9 and M-11 ballistic missiles dominates calculations of the China-Taiwan military balance, but with noticeably less fanfare both sides have begun to supplement their arsenals with cruise missiles. Closely timed Chinese cruise and ballistic missiles attacks would severely tax Taiwanese ground based radars that support their defense of a small number of highly vulnerable airfields.[8]

The already unstable balance of forces between India and Pakistan, too, could be adversely affected by the introduction of cruise missiles and UAVs. According to an Indian report, in early December 2002, a Pakistani reconnaissance UAV violated Indian airspace near the line of control in Kashmir. The flight came immediately after renewed shelling, suggesting that the UAV may have been collecting battle damage information. Additional Pakistani shelling commenced shortly after the Indian side detected the UAV, probably in an effort to divert attempts to shoot it down.[9] These escalations of tensions in Kashmir have been mimicked in the broader arms acquisition domain. Pakistan, for its part, is looking to the United States to sell its army either highly sophisticated *Predator* UAVs or perhaps some less controversial system to replace its own home grown but limited Vision UAV, in order to improve its monitoring of the Kashmiri line of control.[10]

India is even more active in both its own development and foreign acquisition of cruise missiles and UAVs. Its *Lakshya* unmanned target drone, which is thought to be capable of delivering a 450kg payload over a 600km range, will reportedly soon be exported to an unknown country (probably Israel).[11] Israel, in turn, is supplying India initially with two *Heron* long range reconnaissance UAVs, with more to follow, to support its first major UAV base, located at the southern naval command in Kochi.[12] More controversial, due to its potentially unwanted impact on MTCR effectiveness, is India and Russia's co-development of the *Brahmos* dual-mode (antiship and land attack) supersonic cruise missile, capable of delivering a 200kg payload to a range of 300km. Both partners have openly expressed great interest in large export sales of the *Brahmos*. The most provocative development, however, derives from reports that Russia recently has agreed to lease India an *Akula II* nuclear submarine outfitted with 300km range *Club* nuclear-capable cruise missiles. Indian military analysts have already begun to characterize India as possessing a "sea-based nuclear deterrent."[13]

Cruise missiles also figure into tensions in the Middle East. Israel is a major developer of reconnaissance UAVs, has deployed its own *Popeye* air-launched LACM, and has probably deployed nuclear-armed cruise missiles on her submarines.[14] Of course, ballistic missiles played a central role in Iran and Iraq's 1980-88 "War of the Cities." While both countries have on-going ballistic missile development programs, more recently cruise missiles and UAVs have become a part of both nations' missile arsenals. Iran has acquired cruise missile technology—probably from Russia and China—for its own program for developing an antiship cruise missile, called the *Nur*, which comes in both a ground and air launched version. China has also exported various versions of the *Silkworm* antiship cruise missile to Iran; older versions, like the *HY-2* or *HY-4*, could be converted into land attack missiles with ranges of at least 500-700km.[15] Iraq, for its part, has had a long-standing interest in developing LACMs, including a program in the 1980s to convert the Italian *Mirach 600* UAV into an LACM. Evidence is also accumulating that a team of engineers in Yugoslavia is working on a 1,400km range LACM for Iraq, although it reportedly is only in the conceptual stage.[16] More ominous is Iraq's transformation of the Czech L-29 trainer aircraft into unmanned drones capable in theory of flying to ranges in excess of 600km, although Secretary of State Colin Powell told the UN Security Council in February that Iraq had abandoned the L-29 in favor of a home-grown UAV that had been tested on a racetrack flying autonomously for 500km. Such UAVs, outfitted with the kinds of spray tanks that the Iraqis are known to have experimented with, could have devastating consequences were they to deliver biological or even chemical payloads against regional targets, since an unmanned aircraft's flight stability permits it to effectively release and spray biological agent along a line of contamination. While perhaps only 10 percent of a liquid anthrax payload might survive the explosive impact of an Iraqi ballistic missile, nearly the entire capacity of an L-29 spray tank (reportedly containing 300 litres) would be available for dissemination—a factor of 15 better than ballistic missiles.[17]

Defending the Homeland. LACMs and UAVs also have strategic implications for homeland defense. Traditional threat analyses employ "range rings" to show the distance beyond a nation's borders that its missiles can reach. But UAVs can destroy the relevance of "range rings." Cruise missiles or armed UAVs might be launched from concealed locations at modest distances from their targets, or brought within range and launched from freighters or commercial container ships—in effect, a "two stage" form of delivery. The mere fact that a ship launched LACM, fired from outside territorial waters, could strike many of the world's large populations centers or industrial areas, ought to factor into decisions about protecting homeland populations against missile attack. In the aftermath of the 9/11 terrorist attacks, key American decisionmakers have begun seriously to contemplate such threats.[18] Various National Intelligence Estimates (NIEs) have drawn attention to the covert conversion of a commercial container ship as a launching pad for a cruise missile. There are thousands of such vessels in the international fleet; U.S. ports alone handle over 13 million containers annually. Even a large, bulky cruise missile like the Chinese *HY-4 Silkworm*, equipped with a small internal erector for launching, could readily fit inside a standard 12 meter shipping container. Indeed, the latest NIE argues that because such an item, among several others, is less costly, easier to acquire, and more reliable than an intercontinental ballistic missile (ICBM), a cruise missile attack is more likely to occur than a ballistic missile strike.[19]

The offshore option is not the only cruise missile or UAV threat to worry about. Absent more effective controls on autonomous flight management systems, the prospect of converting small airplanes into weapons-carrying UAVs becomes truly alarming. 9/11 provoked a rash of reforms to cope with future terrorist use of a large commercial airliner as a weapon, but these reforms address commercial, not private, aviation. Even though small converted airplanes cannot begin to approximate the effects of using a large airliner, the fact that gasoline, when mixed with air, releases 15 times as much energy as an equal amount of TNT, means that even small airplanes can do significant damage against certain civilian targets. As we have noted, such means are the best method for effectively delivering biological agents. Most important, because such small airplanes could originate from domestically based terrorists—kit-built airplanes do not need a hardened strip to take off—they could be launched from hidden locations in relatively close proximity to their intended targets. The notion that a terrorist group might entertain the use of an unmanned attack means is by no means far-fetched. One recent accounting of terrorist activity notes 43 recorded cases involving 14 terrorist groups where remote-controlled delivery systems were "either threatened, developed, or actually utilized."[20] Such threats may explain in part why MTCR member states agreed at their last plenary meeting in Warsaw, Poland, to strengthen efforts to limit the risk of controlled items and their technologies falling into the hands of terrorist groups or individuals.[21]

The challenges and prospective costs of defending against both offshore and domestic cruise missile threats are enormous. The North American Aerospace Defense Command (NORAD) is currently studying the idea of an unmanned airship operating at an altitude of 70,000 feet and carrying sensors to monitor and detect offshore low flying cruise missiles. Several such airships would be needed together with fast-moving interceptors to cope with perceived threats. An architecture of perhaps 100 aerostats flying at an altitude of 15,000 feet could act as a complementary or alternative system of surveillance and fire control for an interceptor fleet. But additional problems remain. A means of furnishing warning information to the Coast Guard is needed on potentially hostile ships embarking from ports of concern. Sensor data on missile threats must be made able to distinguish between friendly and enemy threats prior to threat engagement. Progress in national cruise missile defense will not occur without corresponding improvements in respective service programs. But the latter efforts lack the necessary funding and are burdened by palpable service interoperability and doctrinal and organizational constraints. The question of affordability looms large: it is safe to say that even a limited defense against offshore cruise missiles would cost at least $30-40 billion, which is never taken into consideration when debate occurs about the costs of national ballistic missile defense. Finally, none of these costs or technical challenges pertains to improved defenses against domestic threats. In the aftermath of the 9/11 attacks, NORAD had no internal air picture; nor were its radar assets linked with those of the Federal Aviation Administration (FAA), which controls internal United States air traffic. Progress toward making such a linkage has occurred, but major holes remain, especially when dealing with detecting low and slow flying air targets.[22] In sum, missile defenses against offshore cruise missiles and domestic terrorist attacks employing small airplanes will remain for at least the next decade operationally and technically problematic, as well as financially taxing. The stress on such defenses will grow worse if UAV proliferation gets out of hand.

Trends in UAV Applications.

UAVs fit importantly into Secretary of Defense Donald Rumsfeld's view of a transformed American military. Upset with the lengthy time it has taken to build up responses to military crises, Rumsfeld foresees a U.S. military that could conduct decisive action with rapidly deployable, agile, stealthy forces able to respond to various contingencies, large and small, with a minimum of logistical support. More important than the number of weapons platforms would be the quality of networking between sensors and weapon delivery systems (or "shooters," in military parlance). The ubiquitous employment of microprocessors throughout military systems; remote sensing technologies (as employed on UAVs); advanced data-fusion software; interlinked but physically disparate databases; and high-speed, high-capacity communications networks, would facilitate the precise delivery of force against the most important time sensitive enemy targets. Sequential fires against these targets, which simply permit the enemy time to recover or hide, would be abjured. Instead, networked sensors and shooters produce simultaneous fires, improving effects by an order of magnitude.

Arming the *Predator* UAV exemplifies this transformation in targeting. A decade earlier, in Operation DESERT STORM, American forces received relatively poor support from overhead reconnaissance and surveillance systems, then the exclusive domain of the national intelligence community. Space-based communications support also produced inadequate results, and such support was critically unavailable to military forces in Somalia in 1993. Circumstances in Afghanistan proved radically different. Operation ENDURING FREEDOM demonstrated the capacity of geographically dispersed forces to perceive simultaneously and substantially the same battlespace. This broadly based battlespace awareness allowed mass effects to be achieved without the necessity of massing forces, thereby reducing vulnerability. Near real time video data from *Predator* and *Global Hawk* UAVs—under the control of military commanders, not the national intelligence community—was relayed via orbiting communications satellites to command centers and individual air controllers on the ground. These air controllers could point their laser binoculars at targets and instantly pass precision bearing and range information (translated into latitude and longitude by a GPS receiver) to command centers and aircraft circling nearby. Combat aircraft armed with Joint Direct Attack Munitions (JDAMs), relatively cheap modifications to existing unguided bombs enabling them to be guided precisely by GPS signals to their targets, could then "reprogram" their bombs to deliver them with remarkable accuracy. Most impressively, this capacity to broaden battlespace awareness through UAVs and space-based communications enabled the America regional commander to direct the battle from his headquarters in Tampa, Florida, while being instantaneously connected to his forward headquarters in Kuwait and a subordinate one in Uzbekistan.

What distinguishes armed UAVs from manned aircraft in such roles is their capacity to loiter on call for periods of 24 hours or more without exposing a piloted and expensive aircraft to enemy fire. As of early November 2002, the U.S. Air Force possessed only about 50 *Predators* and only a small percentage are currently equipped to fire *Hellfire* missiles.[23] The CIA has a small number of armed *Predators*, too, and new versions are being produced at the rate of about two per month. These drones also have several operational weaknesses, including difficulty of flying in bad and icy weather and vulnerability to antiaircraft fire. At least ten *Predators* have perished during missions over Afghanistan or Iraq since the beginning of Operation ENDURING FREEDOM.

Plans are afoot, however, to develop and produce improved versions of the *Predator*. The currently flown model, called the MQ-1B, is powered by a simple reciprocating engine, which propels the UAV at a speed of 80 knots. Propelled by a turboprop engine, a much faster (around 260 knots airspeed) and higher flying version — the MQ-9B, or *Predator B* — has already been built, and three to four more will follow in 2003, with production increasing first to nine and then to 15 annually thereafter. Another version of the *Predator B*, with a 20-foot wing extension, will enable it to stay aloft for 42 hour missions, carrying two external drop tanks and 1,000 pounds of weapons. And while current *Predators* are restricted to carrying *Hellfire* missiles, future versions will carry a variety of more potent weapons, including 250 and 500 pound JDAMs and two different air-to-air missiles. The expected unit cost for newer versions of *Predator* will be double that of the current model, or roughly $4 million.[24] But in view of the *Predator B*'s capacity to dwell on station for nearly 2 days without producing pilot fatigue, refuelling, or wear and tear on limited inventories of advanced high-performance F-15s or F-16s, such armed UAVs are considered a bargain, at least for specialized missions requiring persistent air caps and operating in air defense environments in which manned aircraft would be unduly taxed or vulnerable.

Unmanned combat air vehicles (UCAVs) — armed high performance aircraft that many analysts say could represent the most profound change in the American style of warfare — constitute a potentially valuable but less certain complement to the American military transformation than armed UAVs or more flexibly targeted LACMs. The Pentagon's Defense Advanced Research Projects Agency (DARPA) is currently cosponsoring with the U.S. Air Force a Boeing UCAV prototype, called the X-45A, which had conducted five test flights through the end of 2002. Although the primary stated mission of the UCAV prototype is air defense suppression, others have been mentioned, including delivery of directed energy weapons and even conventional weapons such as JDAMs. At such an early stage in its development, it should come as no surprise that great uncertainty characterizes UCAV development. Some, including the

Secretary of the U.S. Air Force, are concerned that such a highly dynamic mission as air defense suppression requires a pilot and that less active missions such as strategic bombing may be more suitable for future UCAVs. Also muddying the waters are discussions within the Pentagon about merging the X-45A with U.S. Navy requirements into a multi-service UCAV program along the lines of the Joint Strike Fighter project.[25] Close allies of the United States, in particular the United Kingdom (UK), have begun to see a more prominent role for both UCAVs and UAVs. The UK is exploring opportunities to become involved in American UCAV development and has begun a program for its own UAV, called *Watchkeeper*, which has many of the features of the *Predator*. One of several motivating factors driving the UK program is keeping pace with the emerging U.S. doctrine of network centric warfare.[26] Still, UCAVs, as distinct from UAVs and LACMs, are likely to remain a desideratum rather than a practical reality until numerous bureaucratic, doctrinal, and industrial challenges are overcome.

Both technological and policy factors will shape the pace and scope of future UAV prospects. Enormous advances in computer processing power, sensor technology, communications, and imagery processing and exploitation have greatly advanced UAV performance. But technological push is constrained as well as driven by policy considerations. LACMs like the *Tomahawk* languished for nearly 2 decades before they came into prominence during Operation DESERT STORM. Although *Firebee* reconnaissance drones flew thousands of sorties during the Vietnam War, there was a significant lag before the technological leap to the *Predator* was made. Service resistance, determined in part by a continued preference for manned platforms, will remain an important constraining factor. Nevertheless, new requirements for so-called battlefield awareness, increased pressure by the public and political leaders alike to avoid casualties, and technological momentum have converged to accelerate UAV applications.

POLICIES AND POLICY OPTIONS

Cruise missiles have been understood for many decades. But modern UAVs—and especially armed UAVs and UCAVs—were at most on the drawing boards when major international security policies were negotiated. The focus of policy makers on ballistic missiles has also affected the coverage of UAVs in international policies—or the lack of such coverage. Notoriously, UAVs and cruise missiles were omitted from the list of proscribed systems in UN Security Council Resolution 687, the cease-fire terms after the first Gulf War against Iraq. This omission was not fully corrected until the UNSC passed Resolution 1441 nearly 12 years later.

We shall now review four policies (or classes of policies) that could affect future commerce in UAVs. In appropriate cases we shall also discuss policy options. In ascending order of difficulty these policies are (1) Arms control treaties, (2) Export controls in general, (3) the Wassenaar Arrangement (WA), and (4) the MTCR .

Arms Control Treaties.

Armed UAVs and UCAVs did not exist when negotiations were completed for START I (1991),[27] START II (1993),[28] the Treaty on Conventional Armed Forces in Europe (CFE—1990),[29] and the INF Treaty (1987).[30] However, armed UAVs and UCAVs arguably are similar in some respects to cruise missiles and to combat aircraft. And these treaties restrict cruise missiles and combat aircraft.

We cannot pinpoint any current controversies regarding the treatment of armed UAVs and UCAVs by these treaties. However, such controversies would be treated with diplomatic confidentiality if they arose. The Defense Department reviews armed UAV and UCAV programs for treaty compliance.

> Initiatives to modify existing reconnaissance UAVs to deliver ordnance or to develop new unmanned combat aerial vehicles (UCAVs) for flight testing or deployment as a weapon—that is any mechanism or device, which, when directed against any target, is designed to damage or destroy it—must be reviewed in accordance with DOD Directive 2060.1 for compliance with all applicable treaties. Examples of treaties that may be considered include: 1) the 1987 Intermediate-range Nuclear Forces (INF) Treaty, 2) the 1990 Conventional Armed Forces in Europe (CFE) Treaty, and 3) the 1991 Strategic Arms Reduction Treaty (START). As is the practice for all programs, determinations will be made on a case-by-case basis with regard to treaty compliance of armed UAVs or UCAVs.[31]

On theoretical grounds we can identify the provisions of the treaties under which issues might arise.

The START Treaties between the United States and the Soviet Union (later Russia) restrict the numbers of "long-range [over 600 kilometers] nuclear ALCMs." The START I Treaty also restricts "nuclear armaments [on] an aircraft that is not an airplane, but that has a range of 8000 kilometers or more,"[32] identified in the Ninth Agreed Statement as "lighter-than-air aircraft such as balloons, drifting aerostats, and dirigibles."[33] In the event that an armed UAV or UCAV were (1) air-launched, deemed to be a cruise missile, and nuclear armed or (2) lighter-than-air and nuclear armed—it could run into START controversies. However, the distinctions between armed UAVs or UCAVs on the one hand and "cruise missiles" on the other hand, discussed below with respect to the INF Treaty, may mitigate these controversies. An armed UAV or UCAV may, after all, be considered an "aircraft" rather than a "cruise missile." However, this interpretation will not relieve an armed UAV or UCAV of all treaty restraints. The CFE Treaty restricts "aircraft."

The CFE Treaty, between the United States, the Soviet Union, and European states restricts the numbers of "combat aircraft" based in Europe. The Treaty defines "combat aircraft" as "fixed-wing or variable-geometry aircraft armed and equipped to engage targets by employing guided missiles, unguided rockets, bombs, guns, cannons, or other weapons of destruction, as well as *any model or version of such aircraft* which performs other military functions such as reconnaissance or electronic warfare"[34] (italics added). The definition says nothing about whether the aircraft are manned or unmanned. Consequently, and theoretically, this definition could apply to armed UAVs or UCAVs based in Europe. In addition, the italicized language theoretically could apply to other types of UAVs based in Europe. Similar CFE restrictions apply to various types of rotary wing aircraft.[35] But we have seen no indication that unmanned systems were envisioned when the Treaty was negotiated. The CFE numerical limits are high, dating from the last years of the Cold War: 13,600 combat aircraft and 4,000 attack helicopters based in Europe—with various regional and country sublimits. So the restrictions, if any, on armed UAVs, UCAVs, and other UAVs may not be onerous.

The INF Treaty between the United States and the Soviet Union eliminates "ground launched cruise missiles" with a range capability of 500 to 5,500 kilometers and tested as weapon-delivery vehicles. Does it apply to armed UAVs and UCAVs? Arguably, an armed UAV or a UCAV is not a cruise missile; it is recovered after use. Moreover, a UCAV is arguably not "launched"; it "takes off" from a runway like an airplane rather than being launched from a "launcher," which is defined in the Treaty as "a fixed launcher or a mobile land-based transporter-erector-launcher mechanism for launching a GLCM."[36] The range of an armed UAV or UCAV adds another distinction from cruise missiles; the Treaty defines the range capability of a GLCM as "the maximum distance which can be covered by the missile in its standard design mode flying until fuel exhaustion, determined by projecting its flight path onto the earths [sic] sphere from the point of launch to the *point of impact*"[37] (italics added). Because an armed UAV or UCAV does not have a "point of impact," it may not fall into the range restrictions of the Treaty.

All of these treaties have fora in which compliance issues can be discussed. Moreover, the United States can withdraw from any of these treaties on 6 months notice (150 days for the CFE Treaty). But, as discussed above, it is not at all clear that the treaties will ultimately restrict armed UAVs or UCAVs.

On the other hand, we should remember that the legal profession currently is engaged in debating whether the relatively new technology of e-mail messages should be regulated as telephone conversations, letters sent through the postal system, or—in the case of wireless e-mail messages—broadcast media. The even newer technologies of armed UAVs and UCAVs may offer equally fertile opportunities to adapt restrictions similar to those applied to older systems. But the fact that armed UAVs and UCAVs may not have been in the minds of treaty negotiators offers an argument that they are not covered by the treaties at all. They may ultimately be deemed to be neither cruise missiles nor aircraft but rather entirely new systems different from both.

Export Controls in General.

In most governments, export controls are divided into controls on military items and on civil (or dual-use) items. In the United States, the former are administered by the State Department and the latter by the Department of Commerce (DoC).

Up to the present time, UAVs have been largely military—but not exclusively so. Japan, South Korea, and Russia manufacture UAVs for crop-dusting. The United States anticipates an emerging market for UAVs with a variety of civilian applications. Under present export control practices, these "civil" UAVs would be controlled by the DoC or its equivalent in other governments.

This creates a potential security problem. "Civil" UAVs can be used to deliver military payloads. Given the interest of the 9/11 hijackers in crop dusters, any air vehicle capable of dispensing an aerosol is a potential threat. Should such systems be controlled by the DoC?

The controversy over space satellite exports controlled by DoC highlighted the concerns about leaving such controls in an agency devoted to fostering exports. The State Department's export controls generally are regarded as tougher than those of the DoC, which is why exporters favor the latter. The same concerns would be applicable to "civil" UAVs in all governments. The DoC is supposed to refer export applications covered by the MTCR for comments by the Defense and State Departments, but there are exceptions. If DoC denies the export outright, it does not need to be referred; in such case the "no undercut" rule applicable to MTCR decisions (see below) may fail to be imposed. Also, DoC does not require an export license for missile-related exports to Canada—among 98 pages of DoC "license exceptions."[38]

The problem of "civil" exports for which licenses are not required is most acute in "license-free zones." Members of the European Community do not require export licenses for dual-use items traded among themselves. This creates an "Nth exit problem," in which the number of possible exporters increases and the opportunities for unwise exports increase as well.

In the United States, there is a current proposal to move into the State Department the control of all UAVs—military or civil—capable of delivering a 500kg payload to a 300km range. That still leaves lesser "civil" UAVs controlled by the DoC. As the discussion below indicates, these lesser UAVs are the subject of increasing international concern.

So the responsibility for controls over UAVs is likely to be an issue for some time. At present the issue appears to be confined to those nations marketing crop-dusting UAVs. U.S. Government officials can remember no case in which the DoC has received an application for a UAV export.

The Wassenaar Arrangement.

With the end of the Cold War, the structure of export controls directed against the Iron Curtain nations seemed to many to be an anachronism. Those controls were administered by the multinational Coordinating Committee (COCOM), which gave members a veto right on munitions and dual-use exports.

COCOM administered controls on items, such as munitions and electronics, that were still sensitive even in the post-Cold War world and that were not covered by nonproliferation export controls. Therefore, in 1996 a larger group of governments (including Russia) formed a new regime, the Wassenaar Arrangement (WA), to promote "transparency and greater responsibility in transfers of conventional arms and dual-use goods and technologies, thus preventing destabilizing accumulations."

The WA[39] sets out its guidelines in "Initial Elements," revised three times since the original policy, and includes control lists of munitions and dual-use items. UAVs are controlled on Item ML10(c) of the munitions list:

> c. Unmanned airborne vehicles and related equipment, specially designed or modified for military use, as follows, and specially designed components therefore:
>> 1. Unmanned airborne vehicles including remotely piloted air vehicles (RPVs) and autonomous programmmable vehicles;
>> 2. Associated launchers and ground support equipment;
>> 3. Related equipment for command and control.

and also controlled on Item 9.A.12 of the dual-use list:

> 12. Unmanned aerial vehicles having any of the following:
>> a. An autonomous flight control and navigation capability (e.g., an autopilot with an Inertial Navigation System); or,

b. Capability of controlled-flight out of the direct vision range involving a human operator (e.g., televisual remote control).

Note 9.A.12 does not control model aircraft.

These dual-use controls are limited by a "Validity Note" and a "Statement of Understanding":

Validity Note: The control of unmanned aerial vehicles described in 9.A.12. is valid until December 5, 2004, and its renewal will require unanimous consent.

Statement of Understanding: Participating States understand a model aircraft as intended for recreational and competition purposes.

So the WA's dual use controls on UAVs are subject to a sunset clause and may expire in less than 2 years.

UAV technology and associated software also are covered by the WA's controls. Moreover, WA dual use controls are graded at three levels. UAV hardware, in Item 9.A.12 above, is subject to the lowest grade of dual use controls. However, the highest level of dual use controls ("very sensitive") apply to certain UAV software:

9.D.1. "Software" specially designed or modified for the "development" of equipment or "technology" in 9.A. or 9.E.3. of this Annex.

9.D.2. "Software" specially designed or modified for the "production" of equipment in 9.A. of this Annex.

The quotes in the "very sensitive" items refer to terms defined by the WA, and Item 9.E.3. refers to jet engine technology.

What is the net effect of these controls? They are not nearly as tight as the MTCR controls described below. The WA controls basically involve only a requirement to conduct export reviews and to make international notifications. Every 6 months, for deliveries and denials to nonparticipating states, the WA requires notifications of deliveries of munitions items and of denials of the least sensitive (e.g., UAV equipment) dual use items. With respect to exports beyond the participating states of the most sensitive dual use items (e.g., UAV software), the rules require "extreme vigilance," delivery notifications "on an aggregate basis" every 6 months, and denial notifications within 60 days. Participating states are to notify each other within 60 days of an export undercutting a denial notification.

On the other hand, the WA deals with UAVs of very short range, "out of the direct vision range" — a control coverage much more extensive that the MTCR's range of at least 300km. And a January 2003 U.S. proposal to the WA would go further beyond the MTCR by adding, as an "anti-terrorism" measure, controls on kits to convert manned civil aircraft to "poor man's" UAVs:

> PROPOSED TEXT: 9.A.13. Equipment and systems, and specially designed components therefore, designed to convert manned civil aircraft into Unmanned Aerial Vehicles (UAV's) controlled by 9.A.12.a or 9.A.12.b.

The WA's controls may grow in effectiveness as the regime continues to be modified, and UAVs may become increasingly affected by the regime. But this has not happened yet. At present, the lack of strong denial rules and the sunset clause on UAV dual use controls leaves the WA as a second tier of international UAV controls behind the main control policy, the MTCR.

The Missile Technology Control Regime.[40]

The MTCR was announced in 1987 by the G-7 — the United States, Canada, France, the Federal Republic of Germany (FRG or West Germany), Italy, Japan, and the UK. It was a new nonproliferation export control regime to "limit the risks" of nuclear proliferation by controlling transfers that could contribute to unmanned delivery systems for nuclear weapons.

Over the subsequent years, the MTCR's scope was expanded to cover unmanned delivery systems for nuclear, biological, and chemical weapons. And the membership expanded to include all members of the North Atlantic Treaty Organization (NATO), the European Community (EU), the European Space Agency, Australia, New Zealand, Argentina, Brazil, Russia, Ukraine, South Africa, Poland, Hungary, the Czech Republic, and the Republic of Korea. Moreover, Israel, Romania, Bulgaria, and Slovakia have made a political commitment unilaterally to observe the MTCR rules. Other candidates for EU membership, such as Cyprus and Malta, must adopt MTCR controls as part of the EU package but have not yet made a political commitment to the MTCR. China has adopted some elements of the MTCR, but there are troublesome differences between the letter and practice of China's policies and the MTCR.

The regime controls exports for two categories of items. Category I consists of items of greatest sensitivity, which are subject to the most stringent controls. UAVs are covered in Category I, Item 1.A.2.:

> Complete unmanned air vehicle systems (including cruise missile systems, target drone and reconnaissance drones) capable of delivering at least a 500kg payload to a range of at least 300km.

Formulated in the original version of the regime, the 500kg payload was considered the minimum payload for a relatively unsophisticated nuclear weapon, and the 300km range was considered the relevant range for the most compact theaters in which nuclear weapons might be used. Range/payload tradeoffs are taken into account in determining the capability of a UAV, and in 2002 "range" and "payload" were specifically defined. (The definitions were weakened, however, by a regime statement that the determination of range is the sole responsibility of the exporting government.) Category I controls also are applied to production facilities and design and production technology for UAVs with a 500kg/300km capability. Complete guidance sets of a specified accuracy for UAVs—and their production facilities, production equipment, and technology—are also covered under Category I, Item 2.

Category II consists of equipment, components, materials, and technology that, while generally dual use, could make a contribution to Category I systems. For UAVs, these include most of 18 Category II items ranging from jet engines, to composites, to flight control equipment and avionics, to stealth materials and test equipment.

In 1993, in order to cover systems capable of delivering chemical weapons (CW) or biological weapons (BW), using lower payloads than would be needed for nuclear weapons, the regime added (for UAVs):

Item 19.A.2. Complete unmanned air vehicle systems (including cruise missile systems, target drones and reconnaissance drones) not specified in 1.A.2., capable of a maximum range equal to or greater than 300km.

That is, the regime now includes in Category II unmanned systems capable of delivering *any payload* to a range of 300km.

Several levels of rules apply to these items:

Absolute prohibition (until further notice) on the transfer of Category I complete production facilities or the technology for such facilities. It obviously does not make sense to have a nonproliferation regime that allows the creation of new suppliers.

Strong presumption to deny transfers of Category I items. This strong presumption of denial also applies to missiles of any range or payload, or any MTCR-controlled item, for which the purpose is deemed to be the delivery of nuclear, biological, or chemical payloads. Transfers of Category I items may be made. But they are to be "rare" and may only be made if there are (1) binding government-to-government assurances with respect to the end-use and end-user and (2) supplier and not just recipient responsibility for the end-use.

Case-by-case review of export applications for all controlled items.

No-undercut provision according to which MTCR partners will respect each others' export denials or consult before undercutting a denial.

Information exchanges to enforce these rules. And,

Catch-all provisions, observed by most partner governments, under which export reviews will be required for missile-related transfers, whether or not on the MTCR control list, to any destination engaged in Category I programs.

Because, under international law, a policy (such as the MTCR) cannot supersede a treaty, the MTCR's rules do not restrict transfers required by the treaties establishing NATO, the European Community, or the European Space Agency. The license-free zone established within the European Community for dual use transfers allows free trade in many Catgory II items within the Community. In addition, there is a diversity of practices with respect to transfers among MTCR partners. For instance, in 1989 the British established an Open General Export License, waiving the requirement for case-by-case reviews of dual use Category II transfers to other regime members.

The MTCR, which is an export control regime, does not restrict indigenous programs. However, the United States insists that a candidate government forego "offensive" Category I programs (a definition that has become increasingly loose over the years) before it will approve the candidate as a new member. And the MTCR members have synchronized their diplomacy against indigenous missile programs in nations of proliferation concern — leading to a recent 106-nation International Code of Conduct loosely discouraging ballistic missile (but not cruise missile or UAV) programs.

MTCR coverage of UAV technology. The MTCR's control list is revised frequently. With respect to complete UAV systems, the controls have expanded from systems with the 500kg/300km capability (subject to a strong presumption of export denial) to systems of any payload with a 300km range (subject to case-by-case review). A current proposal, for approval under a 6-month "silence" procedure, would expand the Category II coverage to something closer to the WA's "autonomous" and "out of the direct vision range" criteria:

> Item 19.A.3 Complete unmanned aerial vehicle systems, not specified in 1.A.2 or 19.A.2., designed or modified to dispense an aerosol, capable of carrying a particulate or liquid of a volume greater than 20 litres, and having any of the following:
>
> a. An autonomous flight control and navigation capability; or,
>
> b. Capability of controlled flight out of the direct vision range involving a human operator.
>
> *Technical notes:*
>
> *1. Complete systems in item 19.A.3 comprise those UAVs already configured with or already modified to incorporate, an aerosol delivery mechanism. An aerosol consists of a particulate or liquid dispersed in the atmosphere. Examples of aerosols include liquid pesticides for crop dusting and dry chemicals for cloud seeding.*
>
> *Notes:*
>
> 1. Item 19.A.3 does not control model aircraft intended for recreational or competition purposes.
>
> 2. Item 19.A.3 does not control UAVs, designed or modified to accept multiple payloads (such as remote sensing equipment, communications equipment), that lack an aerosol dispensing system/mechanism.

There are other control list expansions that might be appropriate to help limit the proliferation of UAVs capable of delivering nuclear, biological, or chemical payloads:

- Flight control systems for the conversion of manned aircraft to unmanned vehicles (the WA proposal);
- Complete UAVs with a given stealth capability;
- Other UAV penetration aids, such as towed decoys and terrain-bounce jammers specially designed to match the delivery system they are aiding; and,
- A wider range of jet engines, now exempted as being for manned aircraft but suitable for UAV use.

These control list expansions would limit all UAVs — the Category II models (80 percent of all UAVs now on the market) that can deliver any payload to a range of 300km, and the Category I models that can deliver a 500kg payload to that range. The smaller, Category II UAVs are real threats in terrorist hands — delivering kilogram quantities of biological agents — or in professional military hands — saturating defenses.

But the most vexing question concerns the growing use of Category I UAVs for surveillance and, as armed UAVs or UCAVs, combat use.

The problem of large UAVs. Category I UAVs can deliver nuclear payloads or such large quantities of chemical or biological agents that meteorological uncertainties can be swamped. The 500kg (or greater) payloads of such systems can be used to penetrate defenses in a variety of ways — with some payload devoted to penetration aids or, if necessary, with some payload devoted to more fuel to allow on-the-deck flight profiles or round-about routing to approach targets from all azimuths.

The MTCR prescribes "a strong presumption to deny transfer" of such systems. But these systems are in increasing demand. This demand raises the threat that Category I UAVs may become a route to cruise missiles for the delivery of weapons of mass destruction (WMD). But, on the other hand, the demand is currently driven by the use of UAVs to apply military force with great discrimination —

just the opposite of a mass destruction threat. Early in 2002 the administration established a confidential interim policy governing the export of such Category I systems.[41] But what should be the policy over the longer term?

The danger of any loosening of Category I controls—in effect for nearly 16 years—is specifically that of the proliferation of UAVs usable as cruise missiles, and more generally that of a slippery slope with respect to other Category I controls. The next point down the slippery slope would probably be a loosening of controls on space launch vehicles—the hardware, technology, and production facilities of which have long been recognized as being interchangeable with those of long-range ballistic missiles.

Given that the MTCR's current Category I rules allow for some flexibility for "rare" transfers, the cause of nonproliferation would seem best served by retaining these rules and working within them. This would avoid the weakening of a 16-year-old nonproliferation standard and would minimize the risk of slippery slopes that could exacerbate the proliferation problem.

Given the alternatives and the dangers of cruise missile proliferation, only as a last, reluctant resort would nonproliferators want to consider modifying the export rules with respect to Category I UAVs. The basis for such a modification of rules could be to ensure that Category I UAV transfers were substantially more expensive than Category I cruise missile transfers—so that the recipient nation could afford far fewer UAVs than cruise missiles. This is a difficult criterion to meet because, if the MTCR works as intended, some nations might not be able to obtain Category I cruise missiles at any price. But the criterion can be approached by taking advantage of a UAV's extensive infrastructure requirement. A new UAV policy along these lines might read as follows:

> The transfer of Category I equipment for a complete unmanned air vehicle system (Item 1.A.2) may be considered more favorably if all of the following conditions are met:
>
> 1) All of the Guidelines requirements are satisfied, except for the strong presumption to deny the transfer.
>
> 2) The system is not specially designed for internal or external ordnance delivery.

3) The system is specially designed for recovery and reuse.

4) Upon completion of the proposed system transfer, the recipient will have installed full capabilities integrated with the proposed system to:

> A) Command and control system flight and recovery,
>
> B) Retrieve data transmitted by the system, and
>
> C) Analyze the retrieved data.

The only modification of the MTCR's Category I rule would be to "consider more favorably" such a transfer and to be prepared to overcome the "strong presumption to deny." This modification, however, is a change in the central rule of missile nonproliferation; so it would be something to be considered only after trying to live with the less radical alternatives. The modification could be expected to unleash pressures for similar provisions with respect to space launch vehicle transfers. So looser rules on Category I UAV transfers could facilitate both cruise and ballistic missile proliferation.

Moreover, this modification would not ease the transfers of Category I armed UAVs or UCAVs. Given that their purpose is to deliver ordnance, they pose the same proliferation threats as cruise missiles. The policy language for "treating more favorably" UAV exports may only be kicking the armed UAV and UCAV cans down the road. But it is difficult to foresee any reasonably safe way to loosen controls on large armed UAVs or UCAVs.

A safer option—supplementing the policy of working within the Category I rules—might be to develop the UAV industry in a manner similar to that of the space launch industry. This would involve providing "services" but not the transfer of hardware beyond the jurisdiction or control of the state considering a sale. In all but the most advanced nations, many elements of UAV operations—such as satellite imagery for the selection of operating areas and satellite communications for retrieval of data—are already provided on a service rather than an ownership basis. UAV services would extend this principle by having the supplier nation maintain and operate UAVs, while the recipient nation directed the operations and received data gathered by the UAV.

This would be a cultural change for the young UAV industry, but it might make military sense. As Thomas Cassidy, president and CEO of General Atomics Aeronautical Systems, said with respect to the *Predator* system (which is growing over the Category I threshold),

> The last thing [a forward commander] needs is to maintain and operate airplanes. What he needs is intelligence support—somebody looking and then piping video directly to him on a little TV set that we've already made for the special forces people.[42]

Another aerospace veteran, speaking off the record, anticipates that UAV services could be a lucrative business model. Such services would resemble the early and profitable IBM decision to market computer services in preference to hardware sales. UAVs might be painted in the colors of the nation purchasing the services. But the exporting government could retain jurisdiction and control of its UAVs by licensing its own nationals to maintain and operate the vehicles in and over territories approved in an export license.

The Israeli Air Force, as described by a senior defense ministry official, is buying "visint [visual intelligence] by the hour" from a civilian Israeli firm, Aeronautics Unmanned Systems. The firm owns, maintains, and launches an Aerostar UAV, hands it off to military operators when it is over the target area, and retrieves it from the military operators 12-14 hours later. The firm also conducts the entire UAV operation for the Israeli police, turning over to the police only real-time imagery collected by the vehicle.[43]

The U.S. military itself has considered hiring UAV services from a foreign supplier. As of November 2002, PACAF, after losing a satellite that was monitoring Pacific Ocean weather, requested the assistance of the Australian firm Aerosonde for weather-monitoring UAVs. Aerosonde leases such UAVs in units of three for about $700,000—air vehicles, service, and support staff included.[44]

UAV services are analogous, not only to space launch services—which meet the objectives of missile nonproliferation—but also to uranium enrichment services which meet the objectives of nuclear nonproliferation. In both cases, a recipient's insistence on hardware rather than services is a strong indicator of a nefarious purpose. And in both cases multinational institutions, not just national sources, may provide part or all of the service.

There are downsides to UAV services. Some supplier governments might not be assiduous in retaining jurisdiction and control of the vehicles. And, even if the hardware were kept physically secure, technical and operational insights of value for cruise missile programs would almost certainly leak out.

And there is the question whether a contractor would be forbidden to fly a UAV into a combat zone on the grounds that he could become a "combatant in war." The legalities of this would need to be thrashed out. There might be alternatives, such as allowing military personnel from the recipient state to operate imaging shutters or to launch ordnance from the UAV—without gaining hands-on access. Or the supplier state might provide military personnel to manage "combatant functions"—an extension of U.S. Defense Department physical security provided for certain sensitive transfers or U.S. operation of *Patriot* missile batteries on loan.

But the upsides of UAV services are intriguing. Proliferation hazards would be constrained compared to the alternatives. The precedent of looser controls on space launch vehicles could be avoided. The practice of "dumbing down" exports in order to meet nonproliferation constraints might no longer be necessary. Subject to the end-uses approved in export licenses, the benefits of large armed UAVs and UCAVs might be shared with other nations. In short, while meeting the nonproliferation objectives of the MTCR, UAV services would allow the military benefits of the technology to be shared without undue interference from the constraints of the MTCR.

ENDNOTES

1. This paper was originally commissioned by the Nonproliferation Education Center (NPEC) for presentation before a group of U.S. Government officials, Capitol Hill staffers, and press representatives at an NPEC-hosted dinner on March 17, 2003. The authors are grateful for the many comments offered by group participants. This chapter also appeared, in slightly modified form, as an article in *The Nonproliferation Review*, Summer 2003, pp. 66-79.

2. Use of a racetrack configuration suggests that Iraq may not have developed a flight management system for this UAV that would enable completely autonomous flight for the vehicle's full range. Yet, the fact that this UAV possessed a fuel load sufficient to permit such a range suggests that such an autonomous capability existed or was within reach.

3. Gregory DeSantis and Steven J. McKay, *Unmanned Aerial Vehicles: Technical and Operational Aspects of an Emerging Threat,* PSR Report 2839, Arlington, VA: Veridian-Pacific Sierra Research Corporation, 2000.

4. For details on these and other possible proliferation paths, see Dennis M. Gormley, *Dealing with the Threat of Cruise Missiles,* Adelphi Paper 339, Oxford: Oxford University Press for the International Institute for Strategic Studies (IISS), 2001, pp. 17-41.

5. Such results are demonstrated in extensive modeling and simulation of biological attacks. Dr. Gene McClellan, private communication with the author, August 22, 1997.

6. Using entirely off-the-shelf commercial components, the U.S. Navy has one contractor developing a prototype of an "affordable" LACM costing less than $40,000 apiece. "Missiles on a Budget: Navy Meets Home Depot," *New York Times,* December 29, 2002, p. 4, Bu.

7. For a detailed analysis of cruise missile defense, see Gormley, pp. 59-76.

8. For a scenario describing how such a plan might plausibly unfold, see *ibid.,* pp. 48-50.

9. "Pak Spy Plane Intrudes into Indian Airspace," *Jammu Daily Excelsior,* Internet Version-WWW, in English, December 8, 2002 [*Foreign Broadcast Information Service* (FBIS) Transcribed Text].

10. Andrew Koch., "Pakistan Looks to USA to Fill UAV Gap," *Jane's Defense Weekly,* October 2, 2002, p. 5.

11. "India to Soon Export Pilotless Target Aircraft to 'A Foreign Country'," *New Delhi All India Radio Home News Service* in English, December 13, 2002 [FBIS Transcribed].

12. "Kochi to Become Naval Center for UAVs," *Kottayam Mathrubhumi* in Malayalam, December 19, 2002 [FBIS Transcribed].

13. "India: Russia Agrees to Lease Nuclear Submarine," Global Security Newswire, December 2, 2002, available at *www.nti.org.*

14. U. Mahnaimi, U. Conradi, and P. Conradi, "Fears of New Arms Race as Israel Tests Cruise Missiles," *Sunday Times,* London, June 18, 2000, available at *sunday-times.co.uk.*

15. For details on the *Nur* cruise missile, see the *Middle East News Line,* "Iran Reports That It Has Developed a Range of Cruise Missiles," available at *www.menewsline.com/stories/2002/october/10_43_3.html.* For information on converting the *Silkworm* into a land attack missile, see Gormley, pp. 30-33.

16. D. Williams and N. Wood, "Yugoslavia's Arms Ties to Iraq Draw U.S. Scrutiny," *Washington Post,* November 1, 2002, p. A26.

17. "Defending Against Iraqi Missiles," *IISS Strategic Comments,* Vol. 8, Issue 8, October 2002.

18. See, for example, Bradley Graham, "Rumsfeld: Cruise Missile Threat Rises," *Washington Post*, October 18, 2002, p. A1.

19. For a discussion of NIE assessments and the overall impact of the September 11 attacks on missile defense, see Dennis M. Gormley, "Enriching Expectations: 11 September's Lessons for Missile Defense," *Survival*, Vol. 44, No. 2, Summer 2002, pp. 19-35.

20. This accounting is by Victor Mizell, a private security expert and ex-U.S. intelligence officer. See *www.securitymanagement.com/library/001324.html*. The cases include planning by Osama bin Laden to use remote control airplanes packed with explosives to kill leaders at the 2002 G-8 summit in Genoa, Italy.

21. Press Release, "Plenary Meeting of the Missile Technology Control Regime, Warsaw, Poland, September 24-27 2002," at *www.mtcr.info/english/press/warsaw.html*.

22. See Michael Sirak, "US DoD Seeks to Bolster Cruise Missile Defenses," *Jane's Defense Weekly*, September 4, 2002, p. 3, for a discussion of some of the challenges of homeland cruise missile defense. For a discussion of service programs and problems, see Gormley, pp. 61-68.

23. Eric Schmitt, "US Would Use Drones to Attack Iraqi Targets," *New York Times*, November 6, 2002, p. A1.

24. David Fulghum, "*Predator* B to Increase Lethality of UAV Fleet," *Aviation Week & Space Technology*, Vol. 157, No. 20, November 11, 2002, p. 34.

25. Robert Wall, "Uncertainty Engulfs Pentagon's Unmanned Aircraft Plans," *Aviation Week & Space Technology*, Vol. 157, No. 12, September 16, 2002, pp. 27-28.

26. Douglas Barrie, "Britain Determines Military Net Value," *Aviation Week & Space Technology*, Vol. 157, No. 26, December 23, 2002, pp. 53-55.

27. Available at *www.state.gov/www/global/arms/starthtm/start/start1.html#Artl*.

28. Available at *www.state.gov/www/global/arms/starthtm/start2/strt2txt.html#1.0*.

29. Availabl at *www.state.gov/www/global/arms/treaties/cfe.html*.

30. Available at *www.state.gov/www/global/arms/treaties/inf2.html*.

31. OSD, *Unmanned Aerial Vehicles Roadmap 2000-2005*, April 2001, Section 6.4.3, "Treaty Considerations."

32. START I, Article V.19(a).

33. *Ibid.*, hypertext link.

34. CFE Treaty, Article II.1(K).

35. CFE Treaty, Article II.1(L-P).

36. INF Treaty, Article II.4.

37. *Ibid.*, Article VII.4.

38. Available at *w3.access.gpo.gov/bis/ear/txt/740.txt*.

39. Available at *www.wassenaar.org/docs*.

40. Available at *www.mtcr.info*.

41. Amy Svitak, "New U.S. Policy Paves Way for *Predator* Sale to Italy: Move May Narrow NATO Technology Gap," *Defense News*, April 15-21, 2002.

42. David Fulghum, "*Predator*'s Progress: General Atomics is Eying Production of New Lines of Uavs with Improved Speeds, Ranges and Payload-Carrying Capabilities," *Aviation Week and Space Technology*, March 3, 2003.

43. David A. Fulghum, "Israeli Company Is Conducting Surveillance For The Military," *Aviation Week & Space Technology*, June 16, 2003.

44. Perry Sims, "PACAF Considering Leasing Australian UAV," *Journal of Aerospace and Defense Industry News*, November 1, 2002.

CHAPTER 8

GERMAN NUCLEAR POLICY

Ernst Urich von Weizsäcker

Nuclear fission was discovered here in Berlin by Otto Hahn and Fritz Strassmann in 1938, but the first applications were made in the United States. Enrico Fermi's first nuclear reactor began producing small amounts of energy in Chicago as early as 1942, and the first atomic bomb exploded in the Alamogordo desert in 1945.

The Nazi period was the ultimate disaster for Germany (and others). The earlier scientific excellence — bringing more Nobel Prizes to Germany than to any other country during the first third of the 20th century — was badly eroded by Nazi tyranny and criminal anti-Semitism. What the Nazis did not do was done by the War. German industry virtually had ceased to exist in 1945, and almost all cities were destroyed.

The mindset after the war was characterized by guilt, peaceful reconstruction, pacifism (even under the threat of Soviet expansion), and an almost antinational sentiment of "Europeanism." The near absence of patriotism after 1945 was, of course, a consequence of its horrendous abuse by the Nazis but remains difficult for Americans to understand.

Concerning energy policy, two factors were dominant in post-war Europe: coal was the chief source of energy, and demand was rising steeply. The first significant move towards West European integration was the European Community of Coal and Steel (ECCS), founded in 1951. Its six countries, Germany, France, Italy, The Netherlands, Belgium, and Luxembourg, were the nucleus of what 6 years later became the European Economic Community. The ECCS also became a symbol of *industrial democracy*, of co-determination, because for the heavy industries' supervisory boards a one-to-one parity between capital and labor became a mandatory rule, motivated perhaps by the fact that steel at the time was also the core of the arms industry that needed international control.

Not too much later, nuclear energy entered the scene, with France — having almost no coal — taking the initiative. All ECCS countries were happy to agree on a common nuclear power policy for which the European Community of Atomic Energy of 1957 (EURATOM) was founded. Significantly, EURATOM was founded jointly with the European Economic Community and ranking with it at par!

EURATOM had no military arm. This was particularly important for Germany. When the German Chancellor Konrad Adenauer intended to yield to American pressures to join NATO's nuclear weapons program, an outcry of protest swept the country, with a group of 18 atomic physicists, including Otto Hahn, then President of the prestigious Max-Planck-Society, and Werner Heisenberg and Carl Friedrich von Weizsäcker, directors of the Max-Planck-Institute for Physics, leading the protest. They were later called the "Göttingen 18," although only six of them actually resided in Göttingen. The atomic physicists clearly saw the peaceful use of nuclear power as a great hope and were all the keener to keep nuclear energy out of the military odium. In the end, Adenauer had to give in.

Very soon, nuclear power became a technological routine no longer dependent on world class physicists. During the 1960s and 1970s, nuclear power became a centerpiece of industrial renewal and was supported massively by all political parties. The "Limits to Growth" report to the Club of Rome (1972) with its gloomy pictures about resource depletion and environmental pollution, and the energy shock of 1973 added to the feeling that nuclear power was perhaps the solution to a whole range of pressing problems. Similar to the developments in Britain and France, some 10 nuclear reactors were planned during the 1960s and another 15 during the 1970s. Also, nuclear ships were planned. It all looked like an easy run promising formidable profits for the growing nuclear industry. The nuclear industry even suggested doing away with household metering because electricity was going to be so cheap that there would be no point in metering it.

From Wyhl to Chernobyl.

Much to the surprise of the ruling elites, the tide turned against nuclear power during the mid-1970s. The turning point was Wyhl. This wine-growing village on the Upper Rhine facing France was spotted by the conservative provincial government of Baden-Württemberg as a site for a major nuclear reactor. But the government totally underestimated the local sentiments against the plan. Even the thoroughly conservative wine-growers stood up against it. They feared that the water vapor belching out of the cooling towers plus a warmed-up river could cloud the sky and take the sun from their vineyards. In addition, fears of radioactive radiation were spreading. Students from nearby Freiburg University initiated systematic protests and started street blockades against the heavy construction machines approaching the site. Moreover, they created the " *Volkshochschule Wyhler Wald*," a popular, if demanding, "school" of adult education teaching about the steam and clouds problem, radiation, disposal problems, vulnerability of nuclear installations to terrorism and war, solar energy, and energy efficiency.

The coal-dominated state of North-Rhine-Westphalia seized the opportunity of commissioning the Freiburg-based *Ökoinstitut* to write a report on a nuclear-free future for Germany. The Federal Government under Chancellor Helmut Schmidt, however, maintained its full support of nuclear energy, but the popularity of this position was visibly dwindling as the Wyhl protesters gained sympathies throughout the country.

Popular science writer Robert Jungk published *Der Atomstaat* (1977), in which he elaborated on the authoritarian political structures nuclear power would imply.[1] This catapulted the atomic controversy to the level of fundamental questions of freedom and democracy, thus further eroding the support for nuclear power, however peacefully intended.

The nuclear controversies were positively instrumental in the emergence of a new political party, the Greens. (The so-called 5 percent-hurdle that parties must take to enter parliament was meant to and has worked to strongly discourage the creation of new parties.) The Greens were quite radical in many regards, but their unifying theme was opposition to nuclear power in all its forms. They therefore were particularly at odds with the ruling Social Democrats (SPD) under Chancellor Schmidt—from which party many of the early Greens originated. The SPD came into rough times anyway because of the widespread phenomenon of "stagflation" that demoralized Keynesian "liberals" all over the place. Schmidt's junior coalition partner, the Free Democrats (FDP), changed sides and spearheaded neoliberal thinking in the country, helping the conservative Christian Democrats (CDU) under Helmut Kohl to assume power. Thus the Greens inadvertently found themselves in an alliance of opposition with the SPD against the new conservative government, and gradually their views infested the larger partner. Schmidt retreated from party politics while the party moved to the left.

Around 1983, the combined issues of the North Atlantic Treaty Organization's (NATO) nuclear rearmament with cruise missiles and the new "Waldsterben" (forest dieback) brought hundreds of thousands of protesters to the streets and created an atmosphere in which the Kohl government lost the popular majority in opinion polls. Fortunately for him, he had 3 years to go before the next elections, but he felt it was time to act against the steady rise of the Greens. One factor in particular alarmed Kohl and his U.S. friends under President Ronald Reagan: the Greens wanted Germany to step out of NATO, thus making a potential majority of the Greens and the SPD a true spectre for Atlantic defence policy.

Looking at the high popularity of ecological issues, Kohl decided to confront the Greens by putting himself at the top of the environmental movement. This is how Germany under a conservative government became known as an environmental champion and a rather stubborn fighter in the European Union (EU) for stricter environmental standards.

It all happened before the reactor disaster of Chernobyl in April 1986, although some developments were influenced by the Three Mile Island accident. Chernobyl definitively put an end to any plans of expansion of nuclear energy. In the SPD, it shifted majorities and triggered a decision at their party convention at Nuremberg a few months later to completely phase out nuclear power within 10 years. Polls suggested that this decision gave the party a strong and additional popularity push, and that it might take just another 3 years to regain power, together with the Greens, in the federal elections scheduled for 1990.

This prospect, however, made it all the more urgent for Kohl to step up his environmental profile. Immediately after the Chernobyl disaster, Kohl created the new federal Ministry of the Environment (environmental policies thus far had been handled by the Ministry of the Interior.) A year later, in 1987, he appointed a top-class man for the portfolio, Professor Klaus Töpfer, who had served as state environment minister in the Rhineland Palatinate. Töpfer introduced the green dot system for packaging waste and initiated very proactive German and European climate policies. In this, he was backed by an all-party Bundestag commission on climate policy, that boldly demanded a 25-30 percent reduction of CO_2 by 2005.

From German Unification to the SPD-Green Coalition of 1998.

Then came the German unification, in a way Kohl's masterpiece. At the 1990 elections, he was rewarded generously by an impressive victory. The SPD contender, Oskar Lafontaine, and the Greens had made lots of mistakes in the context of the unification, notably by not showing the necessary enthusiasm. (On one important issue, Lafontaine was probably right, namely his strong warning against the 1:1 exchange rate of the East German against the West German D-Mark because this rate implied rapid bankruptcies essentially for all East German firms selling their goods to East European clients paying their dues in Roubles at an agreed exchange rate with the East German Mark. Some analysts see this as the real cause for the nonending tragedy of the German economy after unification!)

Concerning nuclear policy, the unification conveniently allowed Kohl to satisfy antinuclear sentiments by closing down all *East* German reactors and the planned disposal facility at Morsleben.

In the meantime, the climate policy agenda was moved to the forefront of international environmental policies. The adoption at the 1992 Rio de Janeiro Earth Summit of the Framework Convention on Climate Change (FCCC) had an important side effect on nuclear power. It helped keep the nuclear option alive, despite continuing public mistrust. In Germany, the German Physical Society (DPG) significantly was in the forefront of educating the public about the urgency of climate policy, and not a few critics felt that this was a maneuver for a revival of nuclear energy.

Another 4 years of Kohl's administration followed from 1994-98. German industry had urged Kohl to rid himself of Klaus Töpfer who was seen as a liability to industry in the new post-cold-war era of globalization and of relentless cost competition. Kohl did as suggested and gave Töpfer a minor and less controversial portfolio, replacing him by Angela Merkel from East Germany, who at the time had no credits or experience in the field. She actually managed her new field much better than expected and was instrumental in getting the Kyoto Protocol of the FCCC agreed to in 1997.

Concerning nuclear policy, the South German states of Bavaria and Baden-Württemberg, both governed for ages by Christian Democrats (Bavaria by the CSU sister party), felt that the Chernobyl shock was now over and one should return to "reason," i.e., to a further expansion of nuclear energy. But industry placed no new orders for nuclear power plants, and opinion polls showed no signs of new sympathy with the nuclear option. Anyway, the power industry was considerably more hesitant than conservative politicians were in regards the continuation, let alone expansion of nuclear energy.

The "Ausstieg," Perhaps the Most Distinguishing Decision of SPD and Greens.

The federal elections of 1998 brought Kohl's government to an end after 16 years. The SPD campaign included a commitment for a phase-out of nuclear power. The new chancellor, Gerhard Schröder, former premier of Lower Saxony, entered a coalition with the Greens, who had an even stronger view on the phase-out of nuclear energy. Very soon, Schröder, together with Green Minister for the Environment Jürgen Trittin and Economics Minister Werner Müller, entered talks with the nuclear industry and finally found an agreement for a stepwise exit from nuclear power. The talks had been well-prepared by Schröder's attempts to arrive at an energy consensus with industry during his time as premier of Lower Saxony. These talks actually annoyed Lafontaine who wanted the thing done by governmental *oktroi* (decree).

What is the substance of the phase-out, or the "Ausstieg," as it is called in German? In essence, the German Government made an agreement with the electric utilities on a phase-out, with a total amount of 2.623 Terawatthours—of nuclear electricity remaining to be supplied. The utilities are invited to trade the permits allocated to them so as to optimize the economic output. Old reactors needing more maintenance would be retired sooner, while some of the newer ones would continue to operate until the total amount permitted was exhausted. That could be at 2025 or perhaps as late as 2030.

Other parts of the deal were a prohibition on building new reactors, an end to the reprocessing of nuclear materials, and a 10-year moratorium on the exploration of the planned final disposal facility for highly radioactive waste in the salt domes below the Lower Saxony village of Gorleben.[2]

The postponement to a later date of the vexing question of the final disposal of radioactive waste was done at a price. It became necessary to build *intermediary* storage facilities for radioactive waste at each reactor site. The nuclear industry actually welcomed this condition because it helped terminate for the time being the highly controversial and increasingly expensive shipments of radioactive waste on roads or railways. Also, the intermediate storage served to reduce radioactivity and heat production from nuclear waste to some thirty percent of the original intensities, thus dramatically easing the physical specifications for final disposal.

Many Greens and Social Democrats felt the deal was much too generous towards the nuclear industry, while some industry representatives thought it was too ambitious. My own assessment is that is has been a fair deal. It meant that each reactor would be allowed to run for 32 years. Assuming that it takes some 16 years for a nuclear plant to be written off, the owner has another 16 years to make fat profits on it. Moreover, the liberalized electricity markets offered plenty of options to import electricity from abroad. When Edmund Stoiber, the Bavarian Premier and the conservative candidate for the Chancellery in 2002, announced during his campaign that in case of victory he would initiate a revival of nuclear power, it was industry that reminded him that the deal was agreed upon with Schröder, and that there was no intention of ordering new nuclear reactors.

For the Coalition and other ecologically minded people, the deal was ambitious enough to make it politically feasible to adopt a highly proactive renewable energies law (which would have been unrealistic without the time pressure given by the "Ausstieg"). Moreover, the fact that a highly industrialized country felt it could afford phasing out atomic energy altogether has been an extremely strong signal to the international community.

In retrospect, after 6 years of the "Red-Green" government, it can be said that the phase-out of nuclear power stands as the move that distinguishes the government most visibly from the positions of the conservative opposition. (With regard to social and tax policies as well as defense and foreign policies, the reality of the SPD and Greens governance has come very close to what the conservative camp has done and proposed during the past 10 or 20 years!)

Perspectives.

The big question is, of course, whether the Schröder government is right to assume the country can afford the Ausstieg. The time will come undoubtedly, when the replacement problem for nuclear power becomes highly pressing. The surplus capacities of electricity that characterize the European power industry in our days, are certain to disappear within the next 10 years. Rising prices of natural gas have surprised earlier optimists. Wind energy is still on the rise but as yet very far from substituting for nuclear power. So far, all German wind power taken together is worth a mere three nuclear reactors (although the *capacity* may be worth ten or more reactors, but then the wind is not always blowing at optimum speed).

It is hard to believe, therefore, that renewables will be sufficient to close the gap that will be left when nuclear electricity disappears from the market. A more realistic popular option has been the construction of combined cycle fossil power plants using coal and natural gas as fuels. But with the dramatic rise in gas prices, that option is no longer very attractive, and people from all political camps have become more accustomed to supporting renewable sources of energy as the core of the answer to challenge. As a matter of fact, the conservative CDU recently has begun to say that they would like to extend the running time for nuclear reactors in order to leave more time for the build-up of renewable sources of energy.

I am reading with interest that in the United States a new discussion is on-going about a revival of nuclear energy, with an aggressive build-up of new nuclear reactors. Although some groups in Germany may hope for a similar debate in that country, I see it as a marginal minority position. What finds far more support is the more conventional idea of extending the permitted life time for nuclear reactors. Many people from industry are demanding exactly that. But the motive tends to be only that an extended life time would simply take some steam out of the energy debate.

If the nuclear phase-out appears as an irreversible decision, if renewable sources of energy are simply too expensive to be serious candidates for replacing all of today's nuclear plants, what could then be the solution? Leaving out coal, the major cause for the greenhouse effect, I am inclined to think of a systematic worldwide strategy of opening an entirely different option, which tends to be left out and forgotten by mainstream energy planners. It is a systematic approach to increase energy efficiency.

What is that? Essentially energy efficiency or rather energy productivity means to extract more well-being from one kilowatt-hour or from one barrel of oil. Surprisingly, the physics of energy invite speculations of a dramatic improvement of energy productivity. One kilowatt-hour, after all, is enough, to lift a 10-liter bucket of water three times from the sea level to the top of Mount Everest. What we do with one kilowatt hour, is extremely poor by comparison, chiefly because energy is so fabulously cheap.

With my friend Amory Lovins, I dared to put on paper the kinds of technological improvements which are available. In our book, "Factor Four," we feature 20 examples of how to quadruple energy productivity, and some of them actually go much beyond a factor of four.[3]

The main challenge politically will be to make it profitable to go in the direction of aggressively increasing energy productivity. You would not be prepared to carry a 10-liter bucket three times up Mount Everest for anything like the price we pay for one kilowatt hour.

Emissions trading, a revenue neutral ecological tax reform, and desubsidizing energy consuming industrial and transportation activities can lead us a long way towards making energy productivity more profitable.

ENDNOTES - CHAPTER 8

1. Robert Jungk, *Der Atomstaat*, Munich: Kindler, 1977.

2. "Vereinbarung zwischen der Bundesregierung und den Energie-versorgungsunternehmen," *Bundesregierung*, Vom 14, Juni 2000, Berlin, Germany.

3. Ernst Ulrich von Weizsäcker, Amory Lovins, and Hunter Lovins, *Factor Four: Doubling Wealth, Halving Resource Use*, London: Earthscan, 1997.

CHAPTER 9

PRESIDENT BUSH'S GLOBAL NONPROLIFERATION POLICY: SEVEN MORE STEPS

Henry D. Sokolski

More than any other post-Cold War presidency, the Bush administration has emphasized nonproliferation enforcement. Certainly, its actions in the cases of North Korea, Iraq, and Libya have prompted the most significant debate about how to strengthen nonproliferation since India exploded its first bomb in 1974. This window of interest needs to be exploited to strengthen nonproliferation enforcement in as country-neutral a fashion as possible.

Toward this end, the United States has itself proposed a new, tougher set of nonproliferation rules. By far, the most important of these rules are the seven specific proposals President Bush made on February 11, 2004, in an address at the National Defense University (NDU). Properly understood, these proposals recommend a sounder reading of the Nuclear Nonproliferation Treaty (NPT)—one that is true to the NPT's original intent and that deflates mistaken interpretations of the treaty that have enabled North Korea, Libya, Iran, and, earlier, Iraq, to acquire much of what is needed to make nuclear bombs.

President Bush characterized these states' misguided views as a "cynical manipulation" of the treaty. He specifically referred to these states' efforts to twist the NPT's call for the sharing of peaceful nuclear technology into an *unqualified* right to "the fullest possible exchange of equipment, materials and scientific and technological information."

This it clearly is not. As the NPT's first article makes clear, no nuclear weapons state that is a party to the NPT (the United States, Russia, China, France, or the United Kingdom) is permitted to "in any way ... assist, encourage, or induce any non-nuclear weapons state to manufacture or otherwise acquire nuclear weapons or other nuclear explosive devices." Similarly, the NPT's second article prohibits all other members of the treaty from "manufactur[ing] or otherwise acquir[ing] nuclear weapons," and from "seek[ing] or receiv[ing] any assistance in the manufacture of nuclear weapons." Finally, the NPT requires all peaceful uses of nuclear energy to be safeguarded with the aim of preventing their diversion to help make bombs. When the NPT speaks in Article IV about "the inalienable right" of NPT members to develop nuclear energy "without discrimination," it explicitly circumscribes this right by demanding that it be exercised "in conformity" with these articles.

For years, too little effort has been made to define what "in conformity" means. This is what President Bush dealt with in his February 11 address. He emphasized that nations seeking to develop peaceful nuclear energy have no need either for materials that can be used directly to fuel bombs—separated plutonium and highly enriched uranium—or for the uranium enrichment and plutonium reprocessing plants required to produce these materials. As such, he proposed that the world's leading nuclear suppliers of lightly enriched uranium fuel (which cannot be used directly to make bombs) guarantee a steady supply of this fuel to nuclear energy-developing states that are willing to renounce trying to build enrichment and reprocessing facilities themselves. He further proposed that nuclear supplier states should refuse to sell enrichment and reprocessing equipment or technology to any state that does not already "possess full-scale functioning enrichment and reprocessing plants."

Beyond this, the President proposed to strengthen international efforts to interdict illicit nuclear shipments and procurement networks; do more to reduce the accessibility to nuclear weapons-usable materials; and tighten procedures at the United Nations (UN) nuclear watchdog agency, the International Atomic Energy Agency (IAEA). Finally, President Bush urged that within a year, no nuclear supplier should export nuclear equipment to any state that has not yet signed the new, tougher IAEA inspections agreement known as the Additional Protocol.

All of these proposals help give teeth to the NPT's prohibitions against the export and acquisition of nuclear weapons related capabilities and materials. They also constitute a useful extension of the calls by former Presidents Gerald R. Ford and Jimmy Carter nearly 30 years ago to discourage the use of nuclear weapons-usable fuels for commercial purposes.

President Bush's proposals, though, should be viewed only as a start. In fact, several additional measures logically follow from the President's seven proposals and are needed to assure effective nonproliferation. Building on the Bush proposals, the United States, other nuclear suppliers, and like-minded states will also need to:

1. Refuse to buy any controlled nuclear items or materials from new states attempting to develop enrichment or reprocessing plants.

2. Update and strengthen IAEA controls to account for the new ways states could divert peaceful nuclear activities and materials to military purposes.

3. View large civilian nuclear projects with suspicion—including nuclear power and desalinization plants, large research reactors, and regional fuel cycle centers—if they are not privately financed or approved after an open bidding process against less risky non-nuclear alternatives.

4. Demand that states that fail to declare nuclear facilities to the IAEA (as required by their safeguards agreement) dismantle them in order to come back into full compliance and disallow states that are not clearly in full compliance from legally leaving the NPT without first surrendering the nuclear capabilities they gained while NPT members.

5. Support UN adoption of a series of country-neutral rules that track the above recommendations to be applied to any nation that the IAEA and the UN Security Council cannot clearly find in full compliance with the NPT.

6. Starting with the United States, but including Pakistan and India, formally get as many declared nuclear weapons states as possible to agree henceforth to not redeploy nuclear weapons onto any other state's soil in peacetime and to make the transfer of nuclear weapons-usable material to other nations illicit if the transfer is made for a purpose other than to dispose of the material or to make it less accessible.

7. Build on the successful precedent of Libya's nuclear renunciation by encouraging its neighbors—starting with Algeria, Egypt, and Israel—to shut down their largest nuclear reactors.

163

What do these ideas entail? How do they relate to the President Bush's proposals? To answer these questions, each suggestion is examined in turn.

1. *Refuse to buy any controlled nuclear items or materials from or to new states attempting to develop enrichment or reprocessing plants.* One of President Bush's proposals that has already been adopted by the G-8 is that nuclear supplier states not sell fresh fuel to nations that are unwilling to renounce reprocessing or enrichment, and that they refuse to sell any enrichment or reprocessing technology and equipment to states that do not already possess "full-scale functioning enrichment and reprocessing plants." Implementing these rules would certainly help establish a norm against the further spread of commercial reprocessing and enrichment plants. What would be even more effective in deterring new states from developing reprocessing or enrichment, however, would be first to restrict nuclear commercial intercourse with such states by getting the Nuclear Suppliers Group (NSG) membership, and as many other states as possible, to refuse to buy any nuclear commodities or services from them. Second, NSG members should back this rule by making it clear that they will cut off nuclear exports to any state that buys enrichment or reprocessing services or goods from these nuclear entrant nations.

Who would this rule hit hardest? Iran for starters. Nuclear officials there claim that they intend to export reactor fuel from their uranium enrichment and fuel fabrication facilities to other members of the NPT. If the United States is strict about what constitutes "full-scale functioning plants," Brazil and Argentina could also be affected. Brazil is about to launch a commercial enrichment effort at Resende. Officials there concede, however, that their effort would not be able to supply even 60 percent of Brazil's own fuel requirements until the year 2010. They have not even reached an agreement with the IAEA about the proper safeguarding of Brazil's enrichment facility. Still, Brazilian officials have already announced that they intend to export enriched uranium by 2014.

Certainly, if the United States and other like-minded nations grandfather Brazil's enrichment effort as being "full-scale and functioning" while demanding that Iran shut its facilities down, the hypocrisy would be more than just clumsy, it would undermine the credibility of the President's enrichment and reprocessing restrictions for any other country. As for Argentina, it is considering offering reprocessing services to states that buy its large export research reactors.

Neither of these countries' nuclear programs could pretend to be economic without foreign customers. If the United States is serious about achieving the President's goal of freezing the number of states that have reprocessing and enrichment plants, pursuing this complement would be useful.

2. *Update and strengthen IAEA controls to account for the new ways states could divert peaceful nuclear activities and materials to military purposes.* President Bush also backed giving the IAEA more authority to do more extensive nuclear inspection by suggesting that the world's major nuclear suppliers agree to ban controlled nuclear exports to any state that does not sign the IAEA's Additional Protocol for nuclear inspections. Backing the Additional Protocol certainly has merit. The problem with merely backing its adoption, however, is such support fails to address the deficiencies of existing IAEA nuclear audits even with the Additional Protocol. These gaps also need to be addressed.

What are they? The first and perhaps most immediate IAEA shortfall is the agency's lack of near real-time surveillance to prevent the diversion of fresh and spent reactor fuel that could be used to make bombs. IAEA inspectors currently rely on cameras whose "take" of the areas in which fresh and spent fuel are stored is viewed every 90 days.[1] Because these cameras do not have a full view of these storage areas, though, it is possible for would-be bomb makers to divert fresh or spent fuel without the knowledge of the IAEA. If a state has declared or covert reprocessing or enrichment plants, these materials could be converted into weapons usable fuel in a matter of days or weeks—i.e., well before the IAEA could ever know any illicit activity had taken place. To help eliminate this danger, the agency should install real-time full-view surveillance cameras and keep one or more inspectors at the reactor site to keep these cameras running and to report if they should break down.

This, of course, will cost money. The logical parties to foot the bill are the users of the nuclear facilities being inspected. Toward this end, the IAEA's membership should agree to assess an additional fee based on the actual level of use of each of the nuclear facilities being inspected that the users of these plants would be expected to pay in order to remain in full compliance with the IAEA safeguards obligations.

Another IAEA deficiency is its lack of any public record of the special nuclear materials it is supposed to be auditing. In fact, the IAEA does not publish the actual amounts of special nuclear materials it is supposed to be safeguarding, including separated plutonium and enriched uranium that could be quickly converted into nuclear weapons. The net result is that just how much dangerous nuclear material there is and how well it is being guarded is a matter of speculation. The original argument for keeping this information secret was that it might reveal some industrial secret about the production capabilities of particular states. After more than 3 decades of nuclear activity under the NPT and the events of September 11, 2001, this line of argument no longer seems tenable.

Finally, the IAEA needs to reevaluate its current list of direct use materials—i.e., those nuclear commodities that can quickly be converted into bombs and that, therefore, deserve additional inspections and control attention. Currently, the agency's list is limited to highly enriched uranium, separated plutonium, and mixed oxide fuel. Given all the news about Dr. A. Q. Khan's export of uranium enrichment technology and the enrichment programs in North Korea, Libya, and Iran, there has been some discussion of the need expand the list to include uranium hexafluoride—the feed stock for uranium enrichment facilities. It might also make sense to include materials nations might use to boost fission devices: Tritium, lithium deuteride, and helium three.

3. *View large civilian nuclear projects — including nuclear power and desalinization plants, large research reactors, and regional fuel cycle centers — with suspicion if they are not privately financed or approved after an open bidding process against less risky alternatives.* Among the most important of President Bush's proposals were two that would assure fresh reactor fuel exports to nations that renounced attempts to enrich uranium or chemically separate plutonium from spent reactor fuel and ban reprocessing and enrichment exports to states that do not already have "full-scale functioning enrichment and reprocessing plants." As the President noted in his February 11 NDU speech, these

steps are essential to help prevent new states from making nuclear weapons fuel.

This is not because the IAEA or national intelligence agencies can detect covert reprocessing or enrichment activities in a timely fashion. As recent experience with covert enrichment and reprocessing activities in Iran and North Korea demonstrates, they cannot. Nonetheless, it is still important to make new reprocessing and enrichment activities illicit, if only to prevent discovered covert reprocessors and enrichers from legally excusing themselves by claiming—as Iran did—that they merely "forgot" to notify the IAEA of their activities.

Making the mere possession of such facilities illicit would clearly make exposed covert reprocessing and enrichment activities out-of-bounds. Yet, the only surefire technical safeguard against suspect nations quickly acquiring nuclear weapons is to prevent them from acquiring significant amounts of fresh, lightly enriched fuel or from generating significant quantities of spent reactor fuel. Lightly enriched uranium can be fed into a covert enrichment line to make a bomb's worth of highly enriched uranium in a matter of days: Spent fuel can be covertly reprocessed to extract a bomb's worth of plutonium just as quickly. Both spent and fresh lightly enriched fuel are part and parcel of most large reactors' operations. This suggests that rules are needed not only to help make suspect reprocessing and enrichment-related facilities illicit, but to spotlight suspect nuclear reactors as well.

How might this be done? Fortunately, Adam Smith's "invisible hand" of free markets and competition can help. As it turns out, many large commercial nuclear projects and all suspect nuclear projects in less developed nations are demonstrably uneconomical compared to less risky options. Nuclear power and desalinization plants have significantly higher capital costs than their non-nuclear alternatives. In poor, developing countries, the performance of nearly all these plants has been abysmal.

Given the surfeit of isotope-producing research reactors—there are roughly 140 in operation in over 40 countries worldwide—there is scant economic justification for the further construction of additional large research reactors: One can import medical, agricultural, and industrial isotopes from existing machines and send one's scientists to these machines to do research much more cheaply than one can build a large research reactor of one's own. Virtually all of the existing research reactors, moreover, can be converted to run on non-weapons-useable fuels.

As for recent Department of Energy (DOE) and IAEA proposals to create regional reprocessing and enrichment parks, these too are a bad buy. Right now, we have more than enough enrichment capacity to supply lightly enriched fuel to all legitimate civilian reactors. If anything, the lack of demand would suggest the need to further downsize existing enrichment capacity. Reprocessing, meanwhile, is an uneconomical answer to a problem that does not exist: It makes much more sense from a security and economic perspective to store spent fuel in casks and to use fresh reactor fuel rather than to recycle weapons-usable plutonium for civilian reactor use.

What this suggests, then, is a simple tenet: Any large civilian nuclear project that is started before considering safer alternatives in an open international bidding process should be regarded as suspect. Certainly, Iran's power reactor and enrichment activities, as well as North Korea's entire program, Pakistan's import of Chinese reactors, Algeria's large research reactor, and Brazil's proposed uranium enrichment undertaking, would all fail this test. To make this guideline credible, however, the United States and its allies will have to apply it to their own civilian nuclear undertakings as well.

Further federal subsidies and funding of commercial-sized undertakings such as the Westinghouse AP1000, international Generation IV reactor and advanced fuel-cycle cooperation, the advanced hydrogen production nuclear reactor, and the ill-starred $6 billion-plus mixed oxide plutonium disposition program should cease. Such cuts should not be seen as anti-nuclear, but rather as pro-free market. Certainly, if it made sense for Congress and Ronald Reagan to oppose federal funding of such large and potentially dangerous energy projects on economic grounds 20 years ago, it makes even more sense today—after 9/11, the new nuclear security imperatives, and the clear lag in international nuclear demand.

States, of course, are free to do as they please. However, nations that use public funds to support uneconomical nuclear projects should bear the full costs of the risks they are running. Certainly, if they are in debt or need to borrow, they should recognize that their bad investments will be accounted for in the market's determination of their nation's sovereign credit rating. Uneconomical nuclear projects by definition, after all, lose money. More important, they all too frequently tempt their backers to try to make ends meet by selling parts of the project off to whomever is interested, including would-be bomb makers. Brazil whose nuclear program was running in the red in the 1980s, for example, saw advantage in striking a nuclear cooperative agreement with Iraq. Dr. Khan who needed cash and technology to complete a new missile project for Pakistan did the same with North Korea, Iran, and Libya. Pyongyang, meanwhile, also stretched for funds, is sharing it nuclear know-how with Iran. All of these nations are or have been subject to economic or trade sanctions as a result of these transactions. This, in turn, should also highlight the economic costs of pursuing such risky ventures.

4. *Demand that states that fail to declare nuclear facilities to the IAEA (as required by their safeguards agreement) dismantle them in order to come back into full compliance and disallow states that are not clearly in full compliance from legally leaving the NPT without first surrendering the nuclear capabilities they gained while NPT members.* The Bush Administration, by its actions and words in North Korea, Iraq, and Libya, has gone a long way toward establishing the rule that whenever a violating nation fails to properly declare nuclear facilities to the IAEA, it must dismantle them in order to come back into full compliance with its NPT obligations. What the United States should do now is to propose this requirement explicitly.

This would certainly be a helpful, country-neutral rule to have in place when dealing with countries like Iran. The United States should also make it clear that no nation that the IAEA and the UN Security Council is unable to clearly find in full compliance with the NPT will be allowed to leave the treaty legally without first surrendering all the nuclear capabilities it gained while a member of the NPT. The idea behind this is that one cannot enter into a contract, violate it, then announce withdrawal, and not be held accountable for one's misbehavior while a party to the contract.

Some U.S. government legal counsels have objected to this commonsense requirement in the case of the NPT out of fear that adopting such a rule might somehow raise questions about the legality of the United States withdrawing from treaty obligations, such as the ABM Treaty. Their concerns, however, are unfounded: The United States is a law-abiding nation that complies with its treaty obligations. If it takes actions inconsistent with a treaty, it only does so *after* it is no longer a member of the agreement or because it has formally chosen not to be a party. This certainly was the case with the ABM Treaty.

5. *Support UN adoption of a series of country-neutral rules that track the above recommendations to be applied to any nation that the IAEA and the UN Security Council cannot clearly find in full compliance with the NPT.* The idea here would be to take advantage of something that, so far, has frustrated U.S. and allied diplomats — the IAEA's and the UN Security Council's reluctance in making definitive determinations of any nation being in violation and worthy of being sanctioned. Rather than wait upon either of these bodies actually to find a specific country in clear violation of the NPT and then try to get a consensus to sanction, it would make far more sense to delineate in country-neutral terms and in advance what the minimal consequences should be for any country the IAEA and the UN Security Council cannot clearly find to be in full compliance. This approach has the clear advantage of being country-neutral and of forcing the IAEA and the UN Security Council to reach consensus only if they want to prevent action.

6. *Starting with the United States, but including Pakistan and India, formally get as many declared nuclear weapons states as possible to agree henceforth to not redeploy nuclear weapons onto any other state's soil in peacetime and to make the transfer of nuclear weapons-usable material to other nations illicit if the transfer is made for a purpose other than to dispose of the material or to make it less accessible.* One of the most nettlesome nonproliferation challenges President Bush discussed in his February 11 NDU speech was reining in the nuclear proliferation activities of non-NPT states such as Pakistan. Islamabad's blatant proliferation activities technically broke no law. Even worse proliferation, however, is possible: There is reason to worry that a future Pakistan might transfer nuclear weapons to another country. Saudi Arabian officials are reported to be studying how they might acquire nuclear weapons from another country such as Pakistan.

What makes these plans plausible—besides Pakistan's and Saudi Arabia's close security ties—is that they could be carried out legally under the NPT. The treaty, in fact, allows nuclear weapons to be transferred to nonweapons state members (e.g., to nations like Saudi Arabia) so long as the weapons remain under the control of the exporting state. This loophole was explicitly inserted into the NPT in the 1960s by U.S. officials who were anxious to continue deploying U.S. tactical nuclear weapons on NATO's and Pacific allies' soil.

Today, keeping this loophole open no longer looks so attractive. In fact, the United States already has withdrawn its tactical nuclear weapons from foreign allied bases it had in the Pacific, including South Korea, Japan, and Taiwan. The reason is simple: With air- and sea-launched cruise missiles, nuclear-capable carrier-based aircraft, stealth bombers, and accurate submarine-launched and land-based intercontinental ballistic missiles available to quickly deliver nuclear weapons, there is no longer any U.S. or allied need to base tactical nuclear weapons on foreign soil.

The United States is now withdrawing much of its military from Europe. As these troops are withdrawn and as concerns about nuclear terrorism and proliferation grow, the rationale for keeping U.S. tactical nuclear weapons in places like Germany will become weaker, and the desire to prevent other states from redeploying their nuclear weapons onto other states' soil will increase. To address this concern, it would be useful to close the loophole in the NPT that allows this.

The question is how. Some have suggested that we simply make these nations nuclear weapons state members of the NPT. The problem with this approach is that such a move would appear to reward states that have stayed out of the treaty and violated its tenets. A sensible alternative would be for the United States to work with as many nuclear weapons states as possible to get a formal agreement that, henceforth, no nation will redeploy nuclear weapons onto another nation's soil during peacetime. The United States could also try to get other nuclear weapons states to agree to make the redeployment of such weapons or the transfer of nuclear weapons-usable materials illicit so long as the transfer was for purposes other than disposing of these materials or making them less accessible. Such a proposal might usefully be raised in the context of upcoming talks with the

Indian government regarding President Bush's promised reopening of U.S. nuclear cooperation.

Certainly, if the United States agreed to impose such limits on itself, it could help persuade other nuclear weapons states – including those that have not yet signed the NPT – to agree to do so as well. One also could match such diplomatic efforts with initiatives to get as many nonweapons states as possible to agree not to *receive* nuclear weapons in peacetime.

7. *Build on the successful precedent of Libya's nuclear renunciation by encouraging its neighbors – starting with Algeria, Egypt and Israel – to shut down their largest nuclear reactors.* President Bush rightly has spotlighted the success he has had in getting Libya to renounce its nuclear weapons program. The challenge now is figuring out how to establish this precedent as a practical nonproliferation standard that can be applied again in at least one other case. In this regard, neither North Korea nor Iran seem particularly promising prospects, since they are resisting cooperation – much less denuclearization.

The prospects, on the other hand, look much better closer to Libya itself. Specifically, now that Tripoli no longer has a nuclear program, it would seem reasonable for its neighbors to reciprocate by at least shutting down their largest nuclear plants.

Questions have been raised about Algeria's need for a second large research reactor. This reactor can make nearly a bomb's worth of plutonium per year; is located at a distant, isolated site; is surrounded by air defenses; and only makes sense if it is intended to make bombs. In fact, Algeria already has a second, smaller, less threatening research reactor in Algiers. Shutting down the larger plant at Ain Ousseara would save Algeria money and make everyone breathe easier.

Additionally, there is Egypt's large research reactor purchased from Argentina. It, too, can make nearly a bomb's worth of plutonium annually. Perhaps Egypt could offer to mothball this plant in exchange for Israel shutting down its large plutonium production reactor at Dimona. The latter is quite old and will require hundreds of millions of dollars to refurbish. Israeli critics opposed to the continuing operation of the Dimona reactor have publicly called for its shutdown in the Knesset.

Certainly, progress on any of these fronts would be helpful in addressing other proliferation problems in the Persian Gulf and elsewhere. At a minimum, they would help isolate Iran's nuclear misbehavior and establish a stricter norm that for the time being, no nation in the Middle East should operate a large reactor or commercial sized nuclear facility of any kind.

The point here, as with the other proposals above, is to build on the clear nonproliferation successes we now have. Certainly, if we do, we will be safer. If we do not, it is just as certain that we will be buying far more trouble than we can afford.

ENDNOTES - CHAPTER 9

1. One of the ironies of the IAEA's current efforts to promote adoption of the Additional Protocol is that the agency is offering to reduce the number of times it will review its camera takes of fresh fuel storage areas to once a year for those nations it has determined do not have a covert nuclear weapons program. Given the intelligence surprises regarding covert enrichment activities that have taken place in Iran, Iraq, Libya, South Korea, and North Korea, one would think the agency would want to increase its inspections of such fuel.

ABOUT THE CONTRIBUTORS

PATRICK CLAWSON is deputy director for research of the Washington Institute for Near East Policy. His previous positions include 5 years as senior research professor at the National Defense University's Institute for National Strategic Studies; and 4 years each as senior economist at the Foreign Policy Research Institute, the World Bank, and the International Monetary Fund. Dr. Clawson has published op-ed articles in major newspapers including the *New York Times, Wall Street Journal,* and *Washington Post.* In addition to his frequent appearances on television and radio, he has authored more than 30 scholarly articles on the Middle East in such journals as *Foreign Affairs, International Journal of Middle East Studies, Middle East Journal,* and *Les Cahiers de l'Orient.* He has also testified before congressional committees more than a dozen times. Currently serving as senior editor of *Middle East Quarterly,* he was previously editor of *Orbis,* a quarterly review of foreign affairs. Works authored and edited by Dr Clawson include *Eternal Iran: Continuity and Chaos,* coauthor with Michael Rubin (New York: Palgrave, forthcoming in fall 2005), *U.S. Sanctions on Iran* (Abu Dhabi: Emirates Center for Strategic Studies and Research, 1997), *Getting Ready for A Nuclear-Ready Iran,* co-editor with Henry Sokolski (Carlisle, PA: Strategic Studies Institute, 2005) and *How to Build a New Iraq After Saddam,* editor (Washington, DC: The Washington Institute, 2003).

VICTOR GILINSKY is an independent energy consultant and former Nuclear Regulatory Commissioner under Presidents Ford, Carter, and Reagan. He has been active on nonproliferation issues for many years, going back to his early work at RAND in Santa Monica, California. In 1971 Dr. Gilinsky moved to the Atomic Energy Commission in Washington, DC, where he was Assistant Director for Policy and Program Review. From 1973 to 1975, he was head of the RAND Physical Sciences Department. From 1975 to 1984, he served on the Nuclear Regulatory Commission, having been appointed by President Gerald Ford and reappointed by President Jimmy Carter. During his NRC tenure, Dr. Gilinsky was heavily involved in nuclear-export issues. In 1982 he received Caltech's Distinguished Alumni

175

Award. Dr. Gilinsky has a Ph.D. in physics from the California Institute of Technology.

DENNIS M. GORMLEY is a Senior Fellow at the Monterey Institute's Center for Nonproliferation Studies in Washington, DC. He is also a Senior Lecturer on the faculty of the Graduate School of Public and International Affairs at the University of Pittsburgh. Mr. Gormley served for 20 years with Pacific-Sierra Research (PSR) as senior vice president and director of its Washington Operations staff. He also served on PSR's Board of Directors. Mr. Gormley has frequently chaired or served on U.S. Department of Defense advisory committees and frequently furnishes expert testimony to Congress. Before joining PSR in 1979, he was head of foreign intelligence at the U.S. Army's Harry Diamond Laboratories in Washington, DC. Mr. Gormley has published three books, including *Dealing with the Threat of Cruise Missiles* (London: Oxford University Press, 2001) and authored numerous contributions to leading journals and newspapers internationally. Mr. Gormley received a BA and MA in history from the University of Connecticut.

STEPHEN JIN-WOO KIM studied 19th and 20th century diplomatic and military history. At the CNA Corporation, he worked on projects for the U.S. Navy, Marine Corps, and Defense Department. Currently, he is the principal North Korea country analyst at Z Division at Lawrence Livermore National Laboratory. Dr. Kim has briefed the Office of the Vice President, Henry Kissinger, George Shultz, and the Defense Policy Board. He is the author of *Master of Manipulation: Syngman Rhee and the Seoul-Washington Alliance, 1953-1960* (Seoul: Yonsei University Press, 2001) and has authored unclassified and classified articles on the Koreas, East Asia, international security, and military operations. Dr. Kim received his B.A. in history from Georgetown University's School of Foreign Service, writing his thesis on British appeasement policy in the 1930s. After a stint on Wall Street, he earned his M.A. in international security from Harvard University and his Ph.D. in history from Yale University.

MITCHELL KUGLER is Director of Strategic Initiatives for the Missile Defense Systems division of The Boeing Company. He is responsible for leading the execution of Boeing's international missile defense programs with NATO countries, and joined Boeing in 2002 after working 10 years for Senator Thad Cochran of Mississippi, currently the Appropriations chairman. In 2003 Mr. Kugler was a member of a group empanelled by the Assistant Secretary of Defense for International Security Policy to advise the Defense Department on policy options related to the nexus of international missile defense cooperation, export controls, and the Missile Technology Control Regime. Mr. Kugler drafted the National Missile Defense Act of 1999 (Public Law 106-38), which makes it the policy of the United States to deploy a National Missile Defense system when the technology to do so is ready. He also helped draft *The Proliferation Primer*, a 1998 report by the Subcommittee on International Security and Proliferation, and Senator Cochran's September 2000 report, *Stubborn Things: a Decade of Facts about Ballistic Missile Defense*. He was the principal editor for both of these reports. Mr. Kugler also helped plan, organize, and execute the Senate's rejection of the Comprehensive Test Ban Treaty, for which he was a recipient of the National Institute for Public Policy's Security and Arms Control Award for 1999. Mr. Kugler graduated in 1983 from West Point and served in the U.S. Army for 5 years as an infantry officer. He obtained his Master of Arts degree in National Security Studies from Georgetown University in 1992.

HENRY D. SOKOLSKI is the Executive Director of the Nonproliferation Policy Edcuation Center, a Washington-based nonprofit otganization founded in 1994 to promote a better understanding of strategic weapons proliferation issues for academics, policymakers, and the media. He served from 1989 to 1993 as Deputy for Nonproliferation Policy in the Office of the Secretary of Defense and earlier in the Office of Net Assessment and as a legislative military aide in the U.S. Senate. Mr. Sokolski is the author of *Best of Intentions: America's Campaign Against Strategic Weapons Proliferation* (Praeger, 2001), and co-editor with Patrick Clawson, of *Checking Iran's Nuclear Ambitions* (Carlisle, PA: Strategic Studies Institute, 2004).

RICHARD SPEIER served in the federal government in the Office of Management and Budget, the Arms Control and Disarmament Agency, and the Office of the Secretary of Defense (OSD). In OSD he started what is now a 30-person staff to deal with the proliferation threat. Over 10 years he helped design, negotiate, and implement the Missile Technology Control Regime. He is now retired from government service. He is a consultant near Washington, DC, specializing in nonproliferation and counterproliferation. Mr. Speier's recent writings include "MTCR and Missile Defenses: Complementary or Competitive?", *Arms Control Today*, June 2004; and *Nonproliferation Sanctions*, with Brian Chow and Rae Starr, the RAND Corporation, 2001. He has appeared in national and international media; has testified before Congress; and has lectured in the United States, Europe, Israel, and Russia.

ERNST URICH VON WEIZSÄCKER has been a member of the German Parliament since October 1988 and Chairman of the Bundestag Committee on Environment, Nature Conservation, and Nuclear Safety since October 2002. After undertaking interdisciplinary research in Heidleberg for 3 years, he became Professor for Interdisciplinary Biology at Essen University in 1972. From 1975 to 1980 he was the Founding President of the University of Kassel. In 1981 he became a Director at the United Nations Centre for Science and Technology for Development, and then, in 1984, a Director of the Institute for European Environmental Policy (IEEP) in Bonn, London, and Paris. From 1991 to 2000, he was President of the Wuppertal Institute for Climate, Environment, and Energy. For the following 2 years, he was Chairman of the Parliamentary Enquiry Commission "Globalisation of the Economy--Challenges and Responses," and then for another 2 years until 2004, he was a Member of the ILO World Commission on the Social Dimension of Globalisation. He has been a member of the Club of Rome since 1991. Dr. von Weizsäcker studied Chemistry and Physics at Hamburg University and graduated in 1965. He received his Ph.D. in Biology from Freiburg University in 1969.

ALAN P. ZELICOFF is a physician (board certified in Internal Medicine 1992, clinical fellowship in Rheumatology, 1983) and physicist (AB Princeton, 1975), who has had a varied career including clinical practice, teaching, and operations research. In the latter roles, he was Senior Scientist in the Center for National Security and Arms Control at Sandia National Laboratories from 1989-2003. Dr. Zelicoff's interests include risk and hazard analysis in hospital systems and office-based practice, and in technologies for improving the responsiveness of public health offices and countering biological weapons terrorism. He has traveled extensively in countries of the former Soviet Union and has led joint research projects in epidemiology of infectious disease, while establishing Internet access at Russian and Kazak biological laboratories. Dr. Zelicoff is the author of numerous text book chapters and articles in these subjects, and is a frequent contributor to Op-Ed pages in the *Washington Post* and other newspapers. Dr. Zelicoff's latest book is *Microbe: Are We Ready for the Next Plague?* (New York: AMACOM, 2005).